SHE SHALL CRUSH THE HEAD

SPIRITUAL WARFARE FOR WOMEN

NATALYA VAZEMILLER

WESTBOW
PRESS®
A DIVISION OF THOMAS NELSON
& ZONDERVAN

EDITED BY CAROL ERMO
Cover Design by Luke Hochrein lhochrein.art@gmail.com

Unless otherwise noted Scripture taken from the New King James Version. Copyright © 1979, 1980, 1982 by Thomas Nelson, Inc. Used by permission. All rights reserved.

All underlined Scripture is the work of the author.

WestBow Press books may be ordered through booksellers or by contacting:

WestBow Press
A Division of Thomas Nelson & Zondervan
1663 Liberty Drive
Bloomington, IN 47403
www.westbowpress.com
1 (866) 928-1240

Because of the dynamic nature of the Internet, any web addresses or links contained in this book may have changed since publication and may no longer be valid. The views expressed in this work are solely those of the author and do not necessarily reflect the views of the publisher, and the publisher hereby disclaims any responsibility for them.

Any people depicted in stock imagery provided by Thinkstock are models, and such images are being used for illustrative purposes only. Certain stock imagery © Thinkstock.

ISBN: 978-1-5127-1344-2 (sc)
ISBN: 978-1-5127-1345-9 (hc)
ISBN: 978-1-5127-1343-5 (e)

Library of Congress Control Number: 2015915693

Print information available on the last page.

WestBow Press rev. date: 10/23/2015

Contents

This book is dedicated to all wise women of God,
Who want to be obedient only to God,
For they can overcome evil
And bring much fruit to the kingdom of God.
There are still more
Ruths, Annas, Esthers, Sarahs, Leas, Judiths, Deborahs,
Marys, Prescilas, Lidyas,
Mother Teresas, Amy Carmichaels, Katie Davises,
In the making.
Against all odds,
They are going to be persevering in obedience to His Word
And His call on each of their lives.
To be a woman means
To be strong and powerful
And fight in the way God made them.
Yes! Shout praise to the King of kings,
For He knew what He was doing,
When He designed her!

Acknowledgements

ALL THE GLORY IS TO GOD THE FATHER: FOR HIS SON, MOST VALUABLE GIFT TO HUMANITY. FOR HIS SPIRIT, WHICH ENABLED ME TO WRITE THIS BOOK WITH BOLDNESS, AND HIS EQUIPMENT WITH STRENGTH ON DAILY BASIS TO BE OBEDIENT TO THE WORD, PRAY AND FAST.

Also, I thank God for my husband and my two sons, for their encouragement and patience while I was working on the book. I am grateful for all my friends and their encouragement and prayers for this book to come to life.

I am grateful to the Lord for two special people who have been sent into my life to benefit the book: Carol Ermo and Luke Hochrein. Carol Ermo has taken time out of her busy life to look through the manuscript and help me with the editing work. Luke Hochrein has prepared the picture for the book cover.

CHAPTER 1

She Shall Crush the Snake's Head

I

"And I will put enmity between thee and the woman, and between thy seed and her seed; it shall bruise thy head, and thou shalt bruise his heel." (Genesis 3:15 KJV)

*T*he above verse is one of the most profound verses in the whole Bible. Ironically, it is the most misunderstood verse by many Christian clergy and followers of Jesus Christ. In fact, the differences of interpretation of this verse show that the meaning here is deeper than generally has been excepted.

Our true understanding of Genesis 3:15 is very critical for salvation for whole humanity. It especially brings a great significance to Christian women. It carries a liberating and motivational message for womanhood and the importance of the female role in the course of all humanity and salvation of the mankind.

Douay-Rheims Bible (1961) has it this way: *"I will put enmities between thee and the woman, and thy seed and her seed: <u>she shall crush thy head</u>, and thou shalt lie in wait for her heel."*

1

Upon analyzing most versions of Bible translations, I have noticed that the same verse sounds the same to the naked eye. Nevertheless, each translation carries some differences.

The most important meaning of the verse is the one everyone holds at the present. It is the universal belief that it points to Mary and Jesus Christ. It is the most important meaning of a truly remarkable victory in the history of all humanity. It is our liberation from oppression of satan, salvation of our souls and regaining partial rulership over the earth. Jesus has bruised satan on the head through His victory on the cross and taken back from him the keys of hell and death. Now, Jesus has all the authority and has the greatest name. He has given some of this authority to us here on earth. "Behold, I give you the authority to trample on serpents and scorpions, and over all the power of the enemy, and nothing shall by any means hurt you." (Luke 10:19)

In order to have a better understanding of this verse, I have combined all the interpretations of the verse together and come up with the stunning passage which shows exactly what the Holy Spirit has been revealing to me for a long time: ***I am making you (snake) and woman** (and all women) **and your** (snake's) **offspring and her** (and all women's) **offspring enemies and in war like tension, from now on she** (and all women) **is going to be crushing and/or bruising your head, and you are going to look for ways to strike at her** (and other women's and all their offspring) **heel.*** God would take me back to Genesis 3:15 and cause me to pounder the meaning I have never had before, nor was ever looking to see. But His ways are always superb to ours, I have been obedient to work and dig deeper in this verse, the Word, and other observations.

As we can see from the passage, all women are at war and the prime target of satan. Satan is clearly aware of a woman's ability given by God to be at war and strike at his head. It says: 'snake's head, not the tail.' When someone steps on a snake's tail, it has a head to strike the offender. When the snake is crushed on its head, it has no power and loses its ability of defense.

Every woman is at war with the snake. Whether or not she realizes it or not, the snake is quiet busy working against her and her offspring. If every woman will realize her potential, and her mandate to fight the enemy, satan will have very limited power against humanity and in particular every Christian woman's soul, her family and possibly her social circle.

As long as women are blind to their ability and their mandate by God to bruise their enemy in the head; he is going to get away with his dirty ways, tricks and lies with us and our precious children. We can't be ignorant anymore, because many souls are at stake. The enemy's goal is to steal, kill and destroy. Our goal is to fight back and remove his power from him – everything that belongs to God and us and put protective walls from his attacks and advances.

Satan is quiet happy to see that we think of Genesis 3:15 only as of prophesy of redemption through Jesus Christ. He is happy to keep the truth away from us about the power and mandate of every woman to bruise the snake on the head and to train her offspring to do so. He has twisted the truths of certain Scriptures to show limited abilities of women in the church and for the great commission of spreading the Gospel for the salvation of the lost souls. Satan has made most of us believe that our role is only in the home doing child raising and housework. Though, it is our role as women to raise children, be subjective to our husbands and be keepers of our home, our role is much deeper than we all realize. Also, he has made most of us believe that we are limited in understanding the Scripture. Thus, many women have limited themselves to very little involvement with the Word of God. While believing his ideas of our limitations, he has been busy striking the heel of every woman and her offspring from the very minute the words were spoken by God. Unfortunately, many women are not aware of such war and that they have been given by God Himself a great power and ability to crush and bruise the enemy of their souls and family.

In order to know how to act and what to do, we need to know what enmity means. *Enmity* is a feeling or condition of hostility and deep seated hatred. Enmity can be between two beings or parties. To be in enmity is like being in a state of warfare. From Genesis 3:15, we see satan's ability and permission to strike and to war against us and our children. But, we have the authority and ability to defend and bruise him right on his head.

It is very important to know what we are doing or we may make more trouble than benefit. We need to bruise the head, if we miss, the snake can bite us on our heel. Nor should we play with him in anyway. He is a dangerous enemy and knowledge of the Scriptures is very crucial. If we don't do anything, satan is still going to destroy without any opposition from us. Therefore, we have the responsibility to learn Biblical war tactics. As is known, for the lack of knowledge people perish. We can't afford to allow our souls to perish. They are eternal. We need to turn to the Bible to learn God's guidelines and ways to handle the ancient snake with a skill only God can teach and give.

II

From many Bible texts it is clearly seen that woman is made different. She is made physically different. She has different physical and emotional needs. She has a different role in the family and humanity. Therefore, it is not surprising, that God has allowed the woman to crush the snake's head. She is, indeed, able to do just that. She is physically and authoritatively weak compared to the man. Therefore, God has given her the ability to crush where it matters the most – right on the head.

Let's look at woman's abilities in the light of Scripture:

1. *"Then Jael, Heber's wife, took a tent peg and took a hammer in her hand, and went softly to him and drove the peg into his temple, and it went down into the ground: for he was fast asleep and weary. So he died."* (Judges 4:21)

It is very interesting to note that Sisera, the captain of Jabin's army, has been able to survive the battle with many armed and skilled men and run away from Israel's army, just to be put to death by a woman! This is the least he has expected!

2. *"So Abimelech came as far as the tower and fought against it; and he drew near the door of the tower to burn it with fire. But a certain woman dropped an upper millstone on Abimelech's head and crushed his skull. Then he called quickly to the young man, his armorbearer, and said to him, "Draw your sword and kill me, lest men say of me, 'A woman killed him.'" So his young man thrust him through, and he died."* (Judges 9:52-54)

Here we see a woman with an unknown name, who is responsible for saving the tower and lives of many people from burning by Abimelech by striking him on the head!

3. *"And the king said to her, "What do you wish, Queen Esther? What is your request? It shall be given to you – up to half the kingdom!"* (Esther 5:3)

In Esther chp.7, we see queen Esther's petition, before the king Ahasuerus, who later hangs Haman's head instead of Mordecai, her uncle. In chapter 8 & 9, we see a wonderful victory on behalf of the Jewish people. In fact, thanks to Esther's bravery, the whole Jewish nation has been spared from the complete execution and elimination. Haman wanted to hang her relative and has been working on destroying the entire nation.

4. *"So she (the daughter of Herodias), having been prompted by her mother, said, "Give me John the Baptist's head here on a*

> *platter. … And his head was brought on a platter and given to the girl, and she brought it to her mother."* (Matthew 14:8, 11 *words in parenthesis are mine)*

Ironically, so has been the end of John the Baptist, who has given Herodias a hard time about her unlawful marriage to Herod.

5. *"...So the woman said to Joab, "Watch, his head will be thrown to you over the wall." Then the woman in her wisdom went to all the people. And they cut off the head of Sheba the son of Bichri, and threw it out to Joab. Then he blew a trumpet, and they withdrew from the city, every man to his tent. So Joab returned to the king at Jerusalem."* (2nd Samuel 20:21b, 22)

No name is known of this woman, but she is worthy to be mentioned! For her brave and wise act has saved her city from unnecessary loss of lives!

6. *"She went to the bedpost near the head of Holofernes, and taking his sword from it, drew close to the bed, grasped the hair of his head, and said, "Strengthen me this day, O God of Israel!" Then with all her might she struck him twice in the neck and cut off his head. … Then she took the head out of the pouch, showed it to them, and said: "Here is the head of Holofernes, general in charge of the Assyrian army, and here is the canopy under which he lay in his drunkenness. The LORD struck him down by the hand of a woman. As the LORD lives, who has protected me in the path I have followed, I swear that it was my face that seduced Holofernes to his ruin, and that he did not sin with me to my defilement or disgrace."* (Judith 13:6-8, 15, 16 NAB)

According to the book of Judith, Holofernes is a commander in chief of the Assyrian army. No one was able to resist him, except the Israelites. Holofernes has surrounded the city and sieged the land's water supply. Thus, limiting water to the Israelites for thirty four days. There was no escape from death either by dehydration or surrendering to the Assyrians. In order to save her people, Judith goes into the heart of the Assyrian army, where she pleads for mercy. She uses her looks and wisdom to seduce the commander and cut his head. She played very smart and has kept her dignity. With the help of God, she was able to be free of disgrace and do this saving act for her people. In all regards, she didn't act disgracefully and gave no reason to give the men any idea of her being an unrespectful woman. She pretended to be a smart runaway or refugee. Her motive and looks charmed and disarmed the enemy without any weapons.

7. *"And behold, you will conceive in your womb and bring forth a Son, and shall call His name JESUS. He will be great, and will be called the Son of the Highest; and the Lord God will give Him the throne of His father David. And He will reign over the house of Jacob forever, and of His kingdom there will be no end."* (Luke 1:31-33)

And of course, the birth of Jesus Christ through Mary, was the greatest victory! The seed of the woman has grown and become of age. He has done the most damage to the kingdom of darkness. He has taken the keys of death and Hades. He has all authority in heaven and earth, and everything has been made subject to Him. His name is greater than all names. If we are truly His disciples and keep His words, we are given a truly remarkable salvation and His power to protect and destroy the schemes of the darkness against our souls.

III

As you can see, women were executing heads without regular weapons used by men. Their weapons were: wisdom, words, tent peg, a piece of millstone, visit to an enemy camp, a sword, birthing of a son, fasting and invitation to the feast, and a dance. These are just examples of the crushing of a head. There are many more strong stories, where women are used in a powerful way for destruction or restoration. We are women. We are different. We have different abilities than men. We are given an authority to protect against the enmity which exists daily from the day Eve had tasted the fruit of the tree of Good and Evil. We are unique and stunning in our own special way. We can see that being a woman and acting like one is authentic. It is special and unique. God wants to use us differently, because we are made to do things differently from men. Giving up our God's designed femininity and running after a feministic agenda is not the solution. Striving to be like men is only going to rip from us the strength God Himself has given to us. He made us to be women for His reasons and His reasons are more glorious if we accept our womanhood and femininity with gratitude. God can show us how to be us in the way we can be victorious.

God made the woman last in His creation endeavor, as the crown of His creation for a reason! The Bible and human history are full of many references of women, who have made history in a positive or a negative way. Regardless of our awareness, we influence everything around us in one way or the other. Let it be the way with no regrets.

Studying creation narrative, we can see, that the woman was created differently. She wasn't spoken into existence, nor was she made out of dust as the man. "The LORD God formed man of the dust of the ground, and breathed into his nostrils the breath of life; and man became a living being." (Genesis 2:7)

The woman was made by the hands of God out of the living flesh of the man. "And the LORD God caused a deep sleep to fall on Adam, and he slept; and He took one of his ribs, and closed up the flesh in its place. Then the rib which the LORD God had taken from man He made into a woman, and He brought her to the man." (Genesis 2:21, 22) Woman was made last on the list in the creation moment. She has been the crown of God's creation work, before He rested on the seventh day! "And on the seventh day God ended His work which He had done, and He rested on the seventh day from all His work which He had done. Then God blessed the seventh day and sanctified it, because in it He rested from all His work which God had created and made." (Genesis 2:2, 3)

Being made last in the creation moment, can possibly hold a huge significance at 'the end of times' climax. The importance of women in the end of the sixth millennium is crucial. She is the key for harvest of the souls at the fall harvest. Jesus has said to His disciples: "The harvest truly is plentiful, but the laborers are few. Therefore pray the Lord of the harvest to send out laborers into His harvest." (Matthew 9:37b, 38) It is hard to gather the harvest without enough workers. God can use anyone who is willing to work regardless of gender.

The book of Revelation mentions in chapter 12 verses 1&2 about the woman with the child. Even though this sign shows us mostly the timing of God, it is also a God's way to show us the attention to female gender and women's role at the end of human history. Being created last at the end of the sixth day right before the seventh day is of significant importance for us today. We are at the brink of beginning of seven millennium and at the final days of sixth one. It makes one wonder if the order of creation plays any role at the end of time or the day of the Lord. The woman may be indeed a very significant role player at the end. Just as she signified the end of creation, so she signifies and plays an important part at the end of man's kingdom and the beginning of the seventh day or the day of the Lord.

Why woman was chosen by satan as an object for temptation is a true mystery. We may not know it until eternity. One detail is certain – the man gave into temptation with zero resistance. "So when the woman saw that the tree was good for food, that it was pleasant to the eyes, and a tree desirable to make one wise, she took of its fruit and ate. She also gave to her husband with her, and he ate." (Genesis 2:6) When confronted by God, he blamed God for Eve, but not himself. "Then the man said, "The woman whom You gave to be with me, she gave me of the tree, and I ate." (Genesis 3:12) We are not given any information of whether or not Adam has been tempted by the devil prior to this experience. Nor, should we assume that he could have been in the same shoes as Eve, had he been tempted by the devil first. We only know that he hadn't resisted nor raised any question or concern when Eve gave him the fruit.

Can it be that Eve was a point of first temptation attempt because she was the easiest opponent or the strongest one? It is a goal of all battles and wars to get the strongest place and the most important man in the game, then the rest is going to be easier to concur. Adam was the strongest opponent, and the devil needed to tempt and defeat the man. But the devil chose to tempt Eve. Can it be that he saw Eve as his strongest opponent? It is possible, he had thought through to the future and saw something we don't see.

We know from the Bible that the woman is a weaker vessel. The weaker vessel can draw her strength from the Stronger Source, who is going to do the fight for her. We should take heart because, God is with the weak. He actually likes to use weak and insignificant in order to show Himself through them, so the strong cannot take the credit for themselves. God is not going to give His glory to anyone: "I am the LORD, that is My name; and My glory I will not give to another, nor My praise to carved images." (Isaiah 42:8)

Jesus has shown special attention to the women. No other teacher, prophet or any other man of significance has been surrounded by women and has given them so much significance. No other man has been so tolerable of female gender in his midst. Read through all the Gospels and make special note of woman's involvement during Jesus' ministry. He included them in His daily teachings, healings, proverbs, significant events of the New Testament, crucifixion and burial. Jesus has revealed himself to Mary Magdalene first after His resurrection, prior to His ascension to the Father. Women found out about His resurrection before men. It is a great possibility that women were included in His ascension to heaven and the baptism of the Holy Spirit, too.

Both Old and New Testaments include women in stories and instructions. The Lord has made sure to include them in both positive and negative examples. There are also three books named after woman's names: Ruth, Esther and Judith (Apocrypha book).

Reading from the very first chapter of Genesis through last chapter of Revelation, it seems as God has been talking to us and about us, regardless of man's dominant role as a leader in the church and family and man's total dominance and preoccupation with himself throughout the ages.

IV

From day one, the snake has been busy keeping enmity with the woman and her seed. We see devastation of his war throughout the whole history of the humanity. He has been clever in deception and actual physical elimination. He has tried to deceive Jesus and tempted Him in the wilderness. Also, he tried to kill Jesus in infancy. But, he managed to succeed in his plan with little understanding of the cost for himself. He lost at the crucifixion, what have seemed to be satan's victory has become his biggest loss. Satan's cleverness can never overcome God's wisdom. God's ways are above satan's ways and ours. What seems to be a loss to us can actually be a victory. What seems to be a victory to the snake is actually a loss to him. This is good news to us. Not all that seems like a loss is called a loss by God. God's victories are measured with the eyes of eternity.

The enemy leads his enmity tactics through deception and elimination:

- **Deception:** lies and twisted truths about God's laws, truths and His universal moral ethics; false doctrines and religions;

female and male roles; ways of parenting; existence of God, hell and heaven.

- **Elimination:** war, sickness, murder, abortion and birth control.

He uses the following tools for his dirty accomplishments: disobedience to God's Word, breaking of His laws, sin, human body, mind, tongue, eyes, emotions, addictions, needs and wants, mass media, radio, television, internet, books, magazines, billboards, etc. In fact, we have become an easy prey due to our fallen sinful nature, which can't be redeemed or help itself outside of Jesus Christ's delivering and healing grace.

Fruit of satan's enmity:

- *Abortion:* About 1.2 million babies die every year because of abortion. The actual number is greater, because it doesn't account for abortions happening unnoticed from birth control pills and spirals.

- *Human trafficking:* Femicide; sexual exploitation and crimes; intentional harm and limitations of rights to female gender throughout the whole history; the unspeakable crimes in the past and present against women and children, especially of female gender around the world including US; forced marriages especially of minors.

- *Preference male to female offspring:* Preselection abortion in favor of a boy in China, India and other counties; China orphanages are filled with abandoned girls for many years; baby girls abandoned, killed or given into infant/toddler sex slavery as means of elimination; girls do not always get the same medical attention as boys, thus simple preventive measures are often not an option for girls and women. Children of both genders are trafficked, kidnapped, mistreated, and abused.

- ***False religions that have no value of a woman:*** Most world religions have negative teachings against women. (Hence, who is the initiator of those religions, but the snake himself.) This limits their rights as humans, creates the poor treatment, conditions, and ground for human trafficking. On the other hand, the rights of proper respect is the positive achievement of the modern day. False religions put a heavy burden on a woman and strip her of her human rights equal to that of a man in her physical, spiritual and emotional needs. Christianity is the only religion which protects a woman against the extremes of humanism and false religion.

- ***Human sacrifices (especially infants and small children):*** At present and passed, human sacrifices are a very common practice. The most targeted are babies of both genders. Though, humans have been sacrificed at all ages and genders.

- ***War:*** Elimination of a population including men. Unprotected women, elderly and children are the victims. Soldiers on both sides involved in wars are adding to the numbers.

- ***Wrong perception of female role in society:*** Feminism is not a friend to women, because it creates equality in things women are not equally equipped for the tasks. Feminism creates more problems than solutions. It has made women equal to men and created even more confusion in the role of both genders. Thus, unequal heavy yokes are placed on her under which she suffers greatly. Because, in reality she is still a woman and her role and the strength of her gender hasn't changed to handle the modern day demand of equality to a man.

- ***All forms of media:*** Media of all form can produce wonders and positive usefulness. But in the hands of fallen humanity it is used by the enemy to produce deception of all sorts. We are being brainwashed and bombarded daily by media about the way we should be, act, think, look, live, believe, etc. Information is power. But not all information is useful and truthful. Often it can spread poisons like cancer that allow entire nations and generations to rot in their own shame. Society is being literally forced by the devil to think the way he wants them to think and fall into bondage of wrong thinking.

- ***Pornography:*** This evil has poisoned and messed up both men and women. Exposer of it at a young age can make a person sick in their mind for the rest of their days. This evil destroys marriages, true love, and creates violence, crimes and sexual abuse to both genders including children.

- ***Education:*** Our schools and colleges are full of indoctrinating lies such as: humanism, evolution, socialism, communism, new age, etc. Our society has been influenced by this education from a young age.

- ***Eternity:*** "Be sober, be vigilant; because your adversary the devil walks about like a roaring lion, seeking whom he may devour. & Then many false prophets will rise up and deceive many." (1 Peter 5:8 & Matthew 24:11) He is seeking souls even out of those, who believe in Christ, being Christian doesn't always means heaven as the final destination.

The ugliness of the enmity that the enemy leads against the women and their offspring (whole humanity and especially children) is not pretty. He is actively searching how to devour anyone he can: men, women and their children. He is a serious opponent who acts in the favor of his hobby: collecting humanity to spend eternity with him and destroying them while on earth. He is busy wanting only to please himself and his selfishness which spills into the hatred for everyone including God.

V

If we don't think satan is our serious enemy, then we are in trouble. Many battles and sports events have been lost to an opponent or other teams because the opposition hasn't been taken seriously. When? When are we going to snap out of our slumber and start having a serious war against the enemy of our souls? When are we seriously going to take our responsibility into our own hands ladies, and start bruising the snake on its' head? No one can do it for us. I can only work where I have been placed. I can't come and win your battle, I have no authority over your domain. But I hope to open your eyes, so you know what to do. It is up to every woman to take things seriously and start acting accordingly. There are many souls at stake: our husbands', our children's, our parents', our siblings', our extended families', our neighbors', our coworkers, and our own souls. If every Christian woman is going to claim her right position according to God's divine purpose, the end outcome can be tremendous. Do we want to be victorious for eternity? Do we want to just make it by? Or do we want to live this life with a difference? No, God doesn't call us to be in the Christian hall of fame list. Nor does God want to make all of us missionaries and send us to Africa or elsewhere. He is calling us to take our stand against the snake where we are. It may require some changes on our part, which are going to produce positive fruit for the kingdom of God.

Let's not underestimate the murdering enmity of our enemy, nor ignore our call and responsibility before God. The ancient snake has dared to try to be like God, and he has stolen our perfect world of no pain and suffering. He has been a murderer from the beginning. His goal of deception has been only to kill. He has stolen our right to truly dominate the earth in God's perfect design and wants to steal our right to live forever. Hell hasn't been made for humans. Now, he steals multitude of souls into the place that has been designed for him and his servants. Enough is enough. God has given us the ability to be victorious over the devil. One obedient godly woman can make a difference. Think of Deborah, Ruth, Anna, Esther, Judith, Mary and many others who have stayed the course of obedience. One disobedient woman can do much damage, too. Think of Jezebel, daughters of Lot, daughter of Herodias, etc. It is a war out there, things need to be taken seriously. The wise woman shall build her house, but the unwise woman is going to tear it down with her own hands. Think if every Christian woman would rise up to the task of fighting the snake's enmity! The results can be revolutionary!

Women can learn from Israel. They are only powerful and able to crush their enemy's head with the Lord's help. We can't do much apart from God. Jesus is our vine and we are His branches. The more we read, study and apply His Word with obedience, the more we understand and know how to win the spiritual war. Pay attention to how Israel has won its' wars and how God interfered for His precious nation. Too bad, they failed, just like us, to remain in obedience to God. Those wars have been won in a very non-combat way. Learning combat tactics of the modern day army may not be beneficial for the women. Learning God's Word will give us more justice. For our enemy is not in flesh and blood, and therefore our tactics are spiritual. We need to come to God and His Word and learn from Him about the spiritual warfare.

Being a weaker vessel is an advantage, for the much stronger Being, God, is on our side and fights for us in the way even a stronger vessel can't. We need to be aware of our position in the light of God and His Word and how we can attain the results we need with His help. We need to return to His Word, learn His laws and build walls around us. Then, move in obedience to Him by following His Word and answering His call on our lives in places where He has planted us. Apart from God and His protection, we are weak. If we are outside of His protection, the snake can strike us on our heel. Then, we are going to be limping. Unfortunately, the venom tends to travel and poison the victim. Therefore, we should not boast nor threat the snake in anyway. Our victory is only in the Lord. It is crucial to know what one does, for this is a spiritual warfare. In this warfare, God is the One who fights for us. We should not take upon us something that is not given to us, nor do mistakes that may hurt us and others.

➢ **CONCLUSION:** There is an enemy, who is actively seeking to do us and our family harm. Every woman can do something to protect herself and her family from the snake's enmity. God is her only ally and strength. The knowledge and obedience to His Word is of great importance.

➢ **WHAT TO DO: 1.** Pray: 'Dear God, please give me wisdom of how to protect myself and my family against the enemy. Teach me everything I need to do in order to be protected and saved.' **2.** Study the Word of God. **3.** Read this book to find out more about ways to protect yourself and family. **4.** Tell others about this book, so other women can join God's army against the enemy. Together we can do greater harm to the enemy's kingdom!

CHAPTER 2

Build Your Spiritual House

I

*"Now there was a day when the sons of God came to present themselves before the L*ORD*, and Satan also came among them. And the L*ORD* said to Satan, "From where do you come?" So Satan answered the L*ORD* and said, "From going to and fro on the earth, and from walking back and forth on it." Then the L*ORD* said to Satan, "Have you considered My servant Job, that there is none like him on the earth, a blameless and upright man, one who fears God and shuns evil? So Satan answered the L*ORD* and said, "Does Job fear God for nothing? Have You not made <u>a hedge around him, around his household, and around all that he has every side?</u> You have blessed the work of his hands, and his possessions have increased in the land. But now, stretch out Your hand and touch all that he has, and he will surely curse You to Your face!" And the L*ORD* said to Satan, "Behold, all that he has is in your power; only do not lay a hand on his person." So Satan went out from the presence of the L*ORD*."* (Job 1:6-12)

The above passage shows a vivid reality of the spiritual world that is closed to our physical eyes and mind. It is very real and to ignore it is like ignoring the law of gravity. When you drop a glass vase it would break into pieces. When you ignore the effects of the spiritual world on us, we will not know how to protect ourselves. We need to put protective walls around ourselves. We see the following from the above passage:

- God is aware of His creation on earth and especially the righteous and upright ones.
- God takes pride in and boast about those who are faithful to Him.
- Satan has access to the earth and keeps close surveillance on all people.
- Satan's aware of God's special people.
- Satan wants harm to come to those who faithfully serve God.
- Satan bargains for our souls and our quality of life.
- God has the final say on everything. It makes sense to petition before God on our behalf. This is where our prayers are more precious than money.
- Satan couldn't do anything to Job because he had a hedge of protection around him.

In the previous chapter of this book we learned that satan has enmity with womankind and her offspring. *"I will put enmities between thee and the woman, and thy seed and her seed: she shall crush thy head, and <u>thou shalt lie in wait for her heel</u>.'* Pay attention to the last words of the verse: *'thou (snake) shalt lie in wait for her heel."* In other words, the enemy of our souls is looking for opportunity to do us harm. If we allow him, he can bargain his way about us. What are the things we can do to protect us? To be protected is the best defense and offence in any war and battle. Leaving the doors open for our enemy is like letting him come and win with our own permission. If one lives in a hostile environment, one must take all precautions not to allow any harm to come one's way. One would check all the doors, windows, and take any means to be safe and be on guard and ready for action at a moments notice. "But know this, that if the master of the house had known what hour the thief would come, he would have watched and not allowed his house to be broken into." (Luke 12:39) If we know that our enemy is seeking constantly for any means to do us harm, we need to know how we can protect ourselves daily. In the physical world we would build a strong wall, lock our windows and all doors and constantly be on the watch. The same applies in the spiritual world. We need to build our fortress within our abilities and God's help.

II

❖ **SPIRITUAL HOUSE:** *"The name of the LORD is a strong tower; the righteous run to it and are safe."* (Proverbs 18:10).

We need to run into that tower. But this tower is only for the righteous. Sinners do not dwell on that tower. For "Woe to him who builds his house by unrighteousness and his chambers by injustice. Now we know that God does not hear sinners; but if anyone is a worshiper of God and does His will, He hears him." (Jeremiah 22:13a & John 9:31) Breaking God's Word is not just dealing with sin and its' punishment. By breaking God's Word, one breaks their protection wall from our enemy in the spiritual realm. God's Word contains laws which when broken can do much damage to people who break them. The sad side of this reality is that it effects not only the guilty but other people around them. Their children are effected the most. When we keep God's Word, the laws within His Word have special protection for us. Keeping His Word and laws is our wall from the enemy. The enemy constantly seeks to break this wall by tempting us into areas where our defense is weakest, so we can break God's Word. When we study the entire Bible we see that God's blessings and promises are always conditional based on the keeping of His Word. The only unconditional promise is a promise of the Messiah Jesus Christ's first and second coming. By keeping God's Word, we keep the safety wall around us. By breaking God's Word and being in disobedience to Him, we break that wall. We become vulnerable when our walls are shaking and have openings. It is an extremely dangerous condition to live in.

"Now Balak the son of Zippor saw all that Israel had done to the Amorites. And Moab was <u>exceedingly afraid</u> of the people because they were many, and Moab was sick with dread because of the children of Israel." (Numbers 22:2-3) So, Balak hired Balaam to curse the people of Israel in hopes of having victory over them. But instead, Balaam blessed them three times. Nothing can curse God's people except one thing: it is the sin they commit. Balaam taught Balak to do exactly the one thing that would make God to go against Israel. Israelites had become their prey by falling into adultery with their women, worshiping their gods and eating things sacrificed to idols. All of these are an abomination to the God of Israel.

This story of Balak and Israel illustrates a picture of reality of what is happening in the spiritual battles. Just as Balak and his Moabites, satan and his servants are extremely uncomfortable with Gods people. God often uses terms like daughter of Israel or Judea, children of Judea, daughter of Zion, harlot, wife, etc. to describe the nation of Israel. He calls His church His bride and wife. He is working with a nation and people who in His eyes are like women. Women are weaker vessels. They need constant protection by someone superior to them in strength, abilities and position. Israel has been weak without God. The only victories they have ever won were because of God. When they have been right with Him, they had nothing to fear. But when they have been outside of their obedience to God they were weak in strength and overpowered by any nation that went against them. For the Word of God has bound and conditioned them to live under His laws.

God has given authority to men and women to subdue the earth and everything that moves and lives on it, that includes birds, fish and spiritual laws, too. In this law, our thoughts, words, and actions are included. Therefore, our thoughts, words, actions, relationships and lifestyles produce positive or negative outcomes. We constantly sow into our personal lives and then into lives of others. There are many laws that God has put into effect, as He created the universe and humans. Through them He governs physical and spiritual aspects of everything. He created the law of gravity, law of mathematics, all laws of physics and chemistry, law of seasons, law of sowing and harvesting, law of authority, etc. If they are broken, we have many negative consequences. If we know them, understand them and act accordingly, many positive outcomes can be produced and life flows harmoniously. We call those outcomes as blessings and curses. Our safety lies in obedience to the Word of God. Disobedience to the Word creates negative outcomes and curses and can even cost us our eternity. We sow all the time, for God has made it the law of sowing and reaping. Our thoughts, actions and words are not in vain, they produce an outcome regardless of our awareness.

We can't be victorious if we continually break God's Word and therefore His laws. For if we do not obey them, we are not going to be successful in bruising our enemy on the head and advance the kingdom of God. Our human nature of actions and words may destroy us without our enemy's effort. He then can just use the rest to finish up. The result can be devastating in the eyes of eternity due to a great loss of human souls forever. God has given us a command to go into the world and preach the Gospel to every creature and to make disciples. We need to actively plant light and salvation around us. Every Christian needs to be useful and positively fruitful for the Lord in the places He has placed us and the abilities He has given us. He is going to ask of us absolutely everything we have done on this earth, we are not going to escape His eyes. "For My eyes are on all their ways; they are not hidden from My face, nor is their iniquity hidden from My eyes. The heart is deceitful above all things, and desperately wicked; who can know it? I, the LORD, search the heart, I test the mind, even to give every man according to his ways, according to the fruit of his doings." (Jeremiah 16:17; 17:9, 10) May we leave a positive trace after us daily.

III

❖ **FOUNDATION:** *"Therefore, <u>everyone who hears these words of Mine and acts on them will be like a sensible man who built his house on the rock</u>. The rain fell, the rivers rose, and the winds blew and pounded that house. Yet it didn't collapse, because its foundation was on the rock. But everyone who hears these words of Mine and doesn't act on them will be like a foolish man who built his house on the sand. The rain fell, and the rivers rose, the winds blew and ponded that house, and it collapsed. And its collapse was great!"* (Matthew 7:24-27 HCSB)

A Christian needs to build one's spiritual house on the rock, Jesus Christ: "Therefore it is also contained in the Scripture, "Behold, I lay in Zion a chief cornerstone, elect, precious, and he who believes on Him will by no means be put to shame."" (1 Peter 2:6) Jesus is our cornerstone and the foundation rock on which one needs to build one's house. "His name is called The Word of God" (Rev.19:13b) Therefore, one must build a house on the Word of God and not anyone else's opinions or any other source. Building of the spiritual house involves daily personal time with the Word of God. The more one digs deeper into the Word, the deeper one gets into the ground to find this foundational rock on which the pillars and walls can be built. The complete building process involves knowledge and application of the Word of God and close relationship with the Writer of the Word, the Holy Spirit. He is capable of doing the necessary work in us. Without studying His Word, we can't build a solid structure, for the Word of God is the primary building material of the whole spiritual house.

Apostle Peter gives us instructions on how to approach the study of the Word: "So rid yourselves of all wickedness, all deceit, hypocrisy, envy, and all slander. Like newborn infants, desire the unadulterated spiritual milk, so that you may grow by it in your salvation, since you have tasted that the Lord is good. Coming to

Him, a living stone – rejected by men but chosen and valuable to God – you yourselves, as living stones, are being built into a spiritual house for a holy priesthood to offer spiritual sacrifices acceptable to God through Jesus Christ." (1 Peter 2:1-5 HCSB) Let's break this verse into three parts:

1. *Rid yourself of all wickedness, all deceit, hypocrisy, envy, and all slander.* It is our job to put these things aside. These things are not for God's child, because they are sins. One must repent of them. In addition, those things are going to interfere with your ability to understands the Word and receive it with the purity of the truth.

2. *Desire the unadulterated spiritual milk:* Use the pure 100% Word of God with no human input like: expert advises, their studies, books, themed studies, etc. **The pure Bible text is enough!!!**

3. *That you may grow by it (milk) in your salvation:* Only then, we will truly start to grow spiritually and into our salvation. The very first time one comes to Christ is one's birth and beginning. But one need to grow into salvation. "For we have become partakers of Christ if we hold the beginning of our confidence steadfast to the end." (Hebrew 3:14) In Russian it translates this way: "For we have become partakers to Jesus Christ, only if we firmly hold our started life to the end." If one thinks that one's salvation is guaranteed, one has a very poor understanding of the Scripture. For Jesus has said, "To him who overcomes I will give to eat from the tree of life, which is in the midst of the Paradise of God."(Revelation 2:7b) The New Testament gives many warnings of the danger of not making it into heaven. There are many deceptions. Jesus has spoken about the narrow path and gate in order to illustrate how difficult it is, indeed. Apostle Paul has written: "... workout your own salvation with fear and trembling." (Philippians 2:12c HCSB) Knowing the ability of human nature enter

into deception, King David has prayed the following, "I have gone astray like a lost sheep; seek Your servant, for I do not forget Your commandments." (Psalm 119:176)

Jesus has said: "You search the Scriptures, for in them you think you have eternal life; and these are they which testify of Me. But you are not willing to come to Me that you may have life." (John 5:39, 40) We need to study Scripture, for we want to have eternal life. We need to be willing to come to Him when we study the Scriptures. Some Jews have studied the Scriptures, but they have refused to come to Him. Their Scriptural writings have foretold of the Messiah, but once He came they did not accept Him and missed His visitation. How ironic?! Can we read the Bible and still miss Him and go to hell? We need to find the Jesus of the Scriptures. On the contrary, we use the Scriptures to modify it to our lives, our liking, and style. We take the Holy Bible and mold it to our liking so it can work for us. Instead, we need to modify ourselves to the Scripture.

We need to change our attitude and return to the Holy Bible. We need to allow it to teach us what it is saying to us. I believe that it is written very simply for everyone to understand including children. It is written to us in several books and different formats for a reason. It should be an interesting piece of literature for us to read. It has history, science, biography, prophecy, letters, law, instructions, poetry, romance, proverbs, songs, wisdom, and entertaining stories. It has the needed counselling, healing, morals, and instructions on relationships, money management, marriage, child rearing, etc. It teaches us about God and origins of earth and humanity. Most of all it tells us how to get saved and not to perish. If we are spending enough time with it, it is going to have answers for all our questions.

I strongly believe that if one lives in obedience to God's Word, one can heal from much pain and hurt. The Word of God is therapeutic to our minds, hearts, souls, bodies, relationships, etc. But it works to heal only with those who want to apply it in their lives and not modify it to cover their deception. It may create some pain before healing and order comes. When one remodels a beaten up house, one does much demolishing, rearranging and sculpting. There may be a need to work on a fallen foundation, broken walls, chipped paint, new plumbing, new flooring, etc. There is much junk and dust to be removed and cleaned up. The final result is a pleasant house for rest and enjoyment.

The Word of God is our spiritual food. God has taken into consideration our different needs for food. There is milk for babies and solid food for the mature. It has main course, drink, desert, bread, meat, spice, salt, honey, etc. The Word of God needs to be eaten daily. It is the food for our soul. If we don't read, we starve. It is impossible to overeat it. Jesus has called Himself the 'bread of life.' When being tempted by the devil, Jesus has answered: "It is written, 'Man shall not live by bread alone, but by every word that proceeds from the mouth of God.'" (Matthew 4:4b)

When we run after knowledge for our mind and starve our soul, we get sick. We combine things in a way that has never been prepared by the Lord. No man-made study can substitute our daily personal involvement with the food God gives us through the Holy Spirit. On the contrary man-made study can take us off our course and often deceive. Nothing should substitute our personal study of His Word. In our days, it is so hard to find 100% pure teaching. Trusting entirely to teachings and teaching materials can be a spiritual suicide.

God has provided us the Holy Bible. We need to return to God's Word and allow the Holy Spirit to teach us one day at a time. Put aside all commentaries and aids. Take a plain Bible of your choice of translation and start reading. (I like KJV and NKJV.) Start to read the New Testament first. Start with Matthew and go in order. Make an effort to put aside all your prior understanding and accumulation of knowledge. Instead, allow the Word of

God with the help of the Holy Spirit to teach and guide you one day at a time. Set aside any man-made rules and approaches of how to go about it, when to read, etc. Instead, listen to guidance of the Holy Spirit.

We are so conditioned by so many things, that we have become enslaved to things that are not good for us. Jesus has come to set us free and give us abundant life. We are told how to eat, exercise, raise children, how to get saved, what saves, what condemns, how to think, how to act, how to believe, how to study Bible, how to etc… Why have we allowed man-made rules to put us back into chains of captivity? We've forgotten how to truly be ourselves and follow the leading of the Holy Spirit and how to listen to the Word of God. We have become captives of wrong ideas about God and salvation. Many are deceived. I have been deceived in many areas, until I allowed the Holy Spirit to lead me into freedom of His Word and His presence. I no longer want to be captive. I want the freedom which I can get only through His Word, obedience and the relationship He dictates to me. I want the God of Israel to be my God. I believe, if we learn to come only to God Himself through His Word and filling of the Holy Spirit, that there can be many more Mosses, Daniels, Elijahs, Samuels, Abrahams, Pauls, and Peters.

When we allow God and Bible to teach us, we are going to be free. Our goal is to be only subject to Christ, not to anyone or anything, even ourselves, otherwise, we become enslaved. The things that control us can become our idols in various degrees. "You were bought at a price; do not become slaves of men." (1 Cor. 7:23)

Most important, we need to be sure we are checking ourselves in the light of God's Word in order to be saved and not condemned. We need to be free from deception which leads us to hell. We should really scrutinize the Word and ourselves, for now is the time. It will be too late for it in eternity. We can't trust our souls to other human beings and their teachings. Our souls are too precious and Someone has provided a way for them to heaven. Let's find this way!

We have a promise from Jesus: "Most assuredly, I say to you, if anyone keeps My word he shall never see death." (John 8:51) He also gives us more direction about how our faith in Him must be: "Then Jesus said to those Jews who believed Him, "If you abide in My word, you are My disciples indeed. And you shall know the truth, and the truth shall make you free."" (John 8:31) Abiding in the Word means observing it, not just reading it and knowing it. Gathering of biblical knowledge doesn't save us. Obedience to God through Jesus Christ is going to enable us to produce the desired fruit for our salvation.

Abiding in the God's Word is to remain in it, to continue in it, to stay in it, to dwell in it, to last in it, and to endure in it! Such abiding guarantees that we are His disciples and are truly saved. 'Abiding in His Word' means doing and living His Word on daily basis.

The Word of God is working with the soul, heart and mind on a spiritual level. It works with an individual for growth into salvation and a mature spiritual inner being. "For the word of God is living and powerful, and sharper than any two-edged sword, piercing even to the division of soul and spirit, and of joints and marrow, and is a discerner of the thoughts and intents of the heart. And there is no creature hidden from His sight, but all things are naked and open to the eyes of Him to whom we must give account." (Hebrews 4:12, 13) No other book, study and even a correct scriptural based sermon can substitute for personal involvement with God's Word. One's goal must be not so much for accumulation of knowledge but for satisfying daily spiritual need of a believer. One may not know all the places, names, and other facts in the Bible, however one may have a much deeper spiritual understanding which only the Holy Spirit is capable of putting into one's soul through reading and obediently applying the Word of God.

"All things are lawful for me, but all things are not helpful. All things are lawful for me, but I will not be brought under the power of any. All things are lawful for me, but not all things are helpful; all things are lawful for me, but not all things edify." (1st Cor. Cor. 6:12 & 10:23) I strongly call everyone to return to pure Scriptures and put aside all other books and studies. Make a fast of nothing but Scripture for a year. Manna was picked up daily. All left overs were rotten by the next day.

IV

Knowledge of the Word of God is very important. Our enemy has used words of God to tempt Eve and was successful: "Now the serpent was more cunning than any beast of the field which the LORD God had made. And he said to the woman, "Has God indeed said, 'You shall not eat of every tree of the garden'?" And the woman said to the serpent, "We may eat the fruit of the trees of the garden; but of the fruit of the tree which is in the midst of the garden, God has said, 'You shall not eat it, nor shall you touch it, lest you die.'" Then the serpent said to the woman, "You will not surely die. For God knows that in the day you eat of it your eyes will be opened, and you will be like God, knowing good and evil." (Genesis 3:1-5) This passage shows us three things:

1. **Lack of knowledge of God's Word:** Eve's knowledge of what God had said: 'You shall not eat it, *nor shall you touch it*, lest you die.' Here is what God said: "Of every tree of the garden you may freely eat; but of the tree of the knowledge of good and evil you shall not eat, for in the day that you eat of it you shall surely die." (Genesis 2:16b, 17) Do you see any difference? God never said, *'nor shall you touch it*, lest you die' – this has been added by Eve.

2. **Satan uses the Word of God to deceive:** Here he uses it in the twisted form: "Has God indeed said, 'You shall not eat of every tree of the garden'?" He used it with Jesus in the right

form. (Read the whole account of satan's way with Jesus in Matthew 4:1-11)

3. **Satan uses truths in order to deceive:** They are usually half-truths. Half-truths are the same thing as half lies. It is a lie because the purpose is to deceive.
   <u>Truth</u>: "For God knows that in the day you eat, of it your eyes will be opened."
   <u>Half-truth</u>: *1.* "You will not surely die." (Yes, they didn't immediately die physically, but spiritual they died instantly.) *2.* "You will be like God, knowing good and evil." (This knowledge has made them like satan.)

Before we move on, please, take a better look at the devil's skill in deception. Read the account on his temptation with Jesus. It is a great possibility that many are deceived, especially in such a time as we live. Jesus has foretold it Himself: "Then many false prophets will rise up and <u>deceive many</u>." 'Prophets' is just a general word to describe: teachers, preachers, writers, prophets, pastors, and our fellow comrades. Deception can come to us through a book, church Bible study, radio program, a song, Christian TV, internet, etc. One needs to know Scripture and live in obedience of the Word of God, praying daily for God to shield them from deception and help them to understand His truth.

The very first woman with 100% brain capability made a blunder with God's only one request! Think of how much we have in our hands when we get our Bibles to read! It is time to get busy, indeed! Today's Christianity has a deficiency of knowledge in the Word of God, while having been absolutely blessed with different versions of the Holy Bible. We have abundant spiritual material on our menu to choose for our platter: study Bibles, reference Bibles, Bible commentaries, Bible studies, Bible dictionaries and encyclopedias, concordances, Bible atlases, books on various subjects and truths, many self-helps, etc. Somehow we are still malnourished. The nutrition from the given food is not being assimilated by our spirits. Actually, we have a great epidemic in these last days – 'a syndrome of scriptural learning disability.' It is a condition of 'always learning and reading and never able to come to the knowledge of the truth.' We are searching for knowledge, but have missed the truth. Jesus calls Himself the truth. "Jesus said to him, "I am the way, <u>the truth</u>, and the life. No one comes to the Father except through Me."" (John 14:6) We are guilty of searching for information and missing the Author.

"For of this sort are those who <u>creep into households and make captives of gullible women</u> loaded down with the sins, led away by various lusts, always learning and never able to come to the knowledge of the truth." (2 Timothy 3:6, 7) We live in the era of information at the just push of a button. One no longer needs to go anywhere even to the library. Besides TV and radio, we have internet connection. We can now view any kind of 'knowledge' and download any book, magazine, etc. The information is right at out fingertips and in our own hands in the form of smart phones. False prophets have entered into our households with their deceiving agenda through mass communications. They have found their prey: '<u>gullible women</u> loaded down with the sins, led away by various lusts, <u>always learning and never able to come to the knowledge of the truth</u>.' We have a huge epidemic among women. They constantly read the Bible, listen to all sort of preaching and teaching, and read many books and studies, but still are not able to understand the truth. For they are loaded down with the sins, led away by various lusts. Christians must die to self, not grow in self-love and love of this world. If we cater to our 'lusts' or desires, we are going to fall, because our desires need to be conformed to God's Word.

V

❖ **FOUR PILLARS:** *"Then God blessed them, and God said to them, "Be fruitful and multiply; fill the earth and subdue it; have dominion over the fish of the sea, over the birds of*

> *the air, and over every living thing that moves on the earth."*
> (Genesis 1:28)

In the verse, we have four hidden physical and spiritual laws:

1. Law of Authority
2. Law of Sowing
3. Law of Multiplication
4. Law of Harvest

These four laws can be summed this way: One gives authority to sow and multiply through thoughts, words and actions, these in return are going to produce fruit which is going to be harvested. "Do not be deceived, God is not mocked; for whatever a man sows, that he will also reap. For he who sows to his flesh will of the flesh reap corruption, but he who sows to the Spirit will of the Spirit reap everlasting life." (Galatians 6:7, 8)

When God speaks, His Word becomes law. When we break His laws, we break our walls of protection. I consider the above four laws as pillars on which, we as Christian women must begin building protective walls of our homes. Jesus is our cornerstone: "For no other foundation can anyone lay than that which is laid, which is Jesus Christ." (1 Cor. 3:11) It is impossible to set those pillars without a proper foundation. Only personal study and time with His Word and Him enables building of our house as a strong tower, which can't be shattered even during the strongest attacks and storms. Obedience to Him is of crucial importance. Let's analyze these four pillars or laws:

1. **Law of Authority:** Everything we plant through thoughts, words, and deeds are being authorized into existence. We allow planting, multiplication and harvesting to take place. God has established several other laws of authority. All authority has limits to its position. Authority creates order. When it is broken it creates disorder. Any authority which

has gone bad turns into dictatorship, it is ruthless in nature with no consideration for the needs of others. Good authority considers the needs of others and shows the way. Authority of landlord over the renter is in the renting contract. If a renter fails to abide by the contract, the landlord is free to act according to the contract. God has authority over Jewish people according to the covenant they both have agreed to. Jesus has authority over His church according to the new covenant written in the New Testament writings. The Church needs to heed them. For He is going to judge her according to His Word.

2. **Law of Sowing:** We sow or plant something all the time both in the spiritual and physical worlds. Our thoughts, words, and deeds are not in vain. Everything is recorded by God. Everything we plant is going to multiply and produce fruit. When we plant anything, we should expect it to grow, multiply and produce fruit. The final product is going to be harvested. When we plant a tomato seed, it is going to grow into a plant. The plant is going to mature and produce several tomato fruits. Depending on the season, soil, and plant variety, it can produce from 3 to 50+ fruits. All of those tomato fruits can produce hundreds of other tomato plants. We should pay attention to our thoughts, words and actions. Do we really want them to take root and produce and multiply?

3. **Law of Multiplication:** "Both thorns and thistles it shall bring forth for you, and you shall eat the herb of the field. In the sweat of your face you shall eat bread till you return to the ground, for out of it you were taken; for dust you are, and to dust you shall return." (Genesis 3:18, 19) Everything we plant is going to multiply, be it our children's lives or the lies we tell. In the fallen world, weeds grow and multiply faster than the good plants. Think of a garden. It takes so much work to grow good crop, but weeds keep on coming and coming. It may take much effort to produce good fruit in one's life and constantly weed out the weeds one is ashamed of. Now we

can have it much easier through God's gift of ability to renew our spirit and mind! Thank You, Lord, for Your Son!

4. **Law of Harvest:** Now, after planting and multiplication, we are going to see our harvest. We are going to harvest our tomatoes and enjoy them in our salad. Also, we are going to see fruit of our womb grow into adulthood. Also, by this time we have harvested many of our thoughts, words and deeds. But the biggest harvest is yet to come. It will be harvested by God as we die. "Blessed are the dead who die in the Lord ... that they may rest from their labors, and their works follow them." (Rev. 14:13 shortened). May we indeed be blessed for producing good works! But woe to us if we do not. There is going to be a final harvest at the end of the seventh millennium: "And I saw the dead, small and great, standing before God, and books were opened. And another book was opened, which is the Book of Life. And the dead were judged according to their works, by the things which were written in the books." (Rev. 20:12)

Those four laws remind me of earth water cycle: it rains, than it evaporates and turns into clouds; then the clouds produce rain and then evaporation begins again. When we gossip, we are going to be gossiped about. When we lie, someone might lie to us. Sexual sin can produce a child and this child needs to be taken care of. Unfortunately, such children often suffer for the sins of their parents. They often grow in orphanages. Orphanages around the world are filled with children whose parents are alive. Many times, once these children grow up, they lead the same lifestyle as their parents. They are most likely going to produce children that will be dropped into institutions. It is a cycle, continuous cycle. Sinners produce sinners. Curse produces curse. An animal births an offspring after its' own kind. Apples are going to produce apples and not peaches. In order to produce a positive outcome, people need to work in those areas.

Musicians need to practice to be musicians. Houses need to be built. Love can overcome evil and only Jesus Christ can break the cycle of curse and sin.

VI

❖ **BRICKS OR BUILDING MATERIAL:** *"Therefore lay aside all filthiness and overflow of wickedness, and receive with meekness the implanted word, which is able to save your souls. But be doers of the word, and not hearers only, deceiving yourselves. For if anyone is a hearer of the word and not a doer, he is like a man observing his natural face in a mirror; for he observes himself, goes away, and immediately forgets what kind of man he was. But he who looks into the perfect law of liberty and continues in it, and is not a forgetful hearer but a <u>doer of the work</u>, this one will be blessed in what he does. If anyone among you thinks he is religious, and <u>does not bridle his tongue but deceives his own heart, this one's religion is useless</u>. Pure and undefiled religion before God and the Father is this: to visit orphans and widows in their trouble, and to keep oneself unspotted from the world."* (James 1:21-27)

Besides the four pillars, which have been established by God at the moment of creation, we have three building blocks which enable us to build our walls: *1)* condition of our heart *2)* choice of our words *3)* our works. They are the material that is going to determine the quality of our building. They are extremely important for the outcome of the quality of the final structure. If they are of excellent and pure quality, the house is going to be strong. If one choses poor quality of thoughts, words and actions as a building material, the house and walls will take shape and quality accordingly: "Now if anyone builds on this foundation with gold, silver, precious stones, wood, hay, straw, each one's work will become clear." (1 Cor. 3:12-13a)

1. **Inner world or heart:** *"Take heed to yourselves, lest your heart be deceived, and you turn aside and serve other gods and worship them. Keep your heart with all the diligence, for out of it spring the issues of life."* (Deuteronomy 11:16 & Proverbs 4:23) Our heart is very important. Inner world or heart is controlled by our mind through our thoughts.

Ephesians 6:10-20 talks about the whole armor of God. We can't put this armor any other place but on our heart and mind. Peter tells to 'gird up the loins of our minds and to be sober.' To be sober not only from actual wine but from spiritual sleep, inactivity and laziness. The enemy uses all his effort to get to our hearts through our thoughts. If he is successful he can do much damage to us and others around us through us, and can even destroy us and them. It seems that everyone talks about positive thinking. Bible has taught it from the beginning. Jesus takes things to a higher level and raises a bar of holiness above the law. The law tells us to not commit adultery, He has said not to even lust. It is enough to be a murderer only by hating a brother: "Whoever hates his brother is a murderer, and you know that no murderer has eternal life abiding in him." (1 John 3:15)

Our thoughts need to be worthy of our name, they need to be Christ like. Our mind must be conformed to the Word of God. All our thoughts need to pass the test of the Word of God. All human battlefields are thought within the heart. The losses and victories in the heart are going to be seen outwardly to the world through the eyes, face, body, words, choices, sanity, works, actions and everything else. A Christian cannot build strong walls out of sinful and abominable thoughts. One's ability to control one's own inner self and thoughts is very crucial for salvation, survival in spiritual battles and positive outcomes in our lives. Through the mind one filters what one plants and reaps. If we submit our mind to God and His Word, we will succeed. Our success is going to be measured by eternity. Only God's eyes and His scales are going to test our success. One should stay clear from what humans describe as success. The Bible instructs us to: "Set your mind on things above, not on things on the earth. For you died, and your life is hidden with Christ in God. "For My thoughts are not your thoughts, nor are your ways My ways," says the LORD. "For as the heavens are higher than the earth, so are My ways higher than your ways, and My thoughts than your thoughts."" (Colossians 3:2, 3 & Isaiah 55:8, 9)

"The fear of the LORD is the beginning of wisdom; a good understanding have all those who do His commandments. His praise endures forever.' (Psalm 111:10) In order to have our thoughts under control, we need to start obeying God's Word. It is impossible to be a master of your mind without application of obedience to His Word. Apostle Paul gives us a very good quick tip of how to get our thought life into the healthy thinking pattern: "Finely, brethren, whatever things are true, whatever things are noble, whatever things are just, whatever things are pure, whatever things are lovely, whatever things are of good report, if there is any virtue and if there is anything praiseworthy – meditate on these things." (Philippians 4:8) If our heart is desiring things and actions contradictory to God's Word, we need to deal with them at once.

The inner world which we call the heart is built by the quality of our thoughts and willingness to conform them to the Word of God. We need to control the information entering our mind. Just as we install a filtration system on our water supply, to avoid its' contamination from a variety of sources. Even the best filtration system runs into overload and potential break down, when it filters water full of dirt, twigs and other garbage. Add to it pesticides and other poisons and it won't be able to filter them for safe drinking. Therefore, we should not let any such junk even near our inner well. We need to avoid places and information that can break our filtration and poison our drinking waters. God can't use vessels with dirty water. Only pure and clean vessel is deemed pleasant to the Lord for use and His pleasure: "A little leaven leavens the whole lump." (Galatian 5:9)

"Therefore, as the Holy Spirit says: "Today, if you will hear His voice, do not harden your hearts as in the rebellion, in the day of trial in the wilderness, where your fathers tested Me, tried Me, and saw My works forty years. Therefore I was angry with that generation, and said, 'They always go astray in their heart, and they have not known My ways.' So I swore in My wrath, 'They shall not enter My rest.'" Beware, brethren, lest there be in any of you an evil heart of unbelief in departing from the living God; but exhort one another daily, while it is called "Today," lest any of you be hardened through the deceitfulness of sin. For we have become partakers of Christ if we hold the beginning of our confidence steadfast to the end, while it is said: 'Today, if you will hear His voice, do not harden your hearts as in the rebellion.' & Blessed are the pure in heart, for they shall see God." (Hebrew 3:7-15 & Matthew 5:8)

2. **Tongue and words:** Jesus has said: "Either make the tree good and its fruit good, or else make the tree bad and its fruit bad; for a tree is known by its fruit. Brood of vipers! How can you, being evil, speak good things? For out of the abundance of the heart the mouth speaks. A good man out of the good treasure of his heart brings forth good things, and an evil man out of the evil treasure brings forth evil things. But I say to you that for <u>every idle word</u> men may speak, <u>they will give account of it in the day of judgement</u>. For by your words you will be justified, and by your words you will be condemned." (Matthew 12:33-37).

In some other translations the word *'idle'* is used as 'careless.' Feel free to look these words up in dictionary. The word *idle* is careless, unproductive, meaningless, and senseless. We all need to bridle our tongue indeed! For if Jesus has said that 'for every <u>idle word</u> men may speak, they will give account of it in the day of judgement', it is going to be so. We seldom pay attention to our words in terms of sin. Many Christians wouldn't steal, murder or commit adultery, but their mouths lead them right to hell. Our words are going to reveal the quality of our inner man. We simply can't fake it. The Word of God tells us so. We may cover the defect of our heart only temporarily, but eventually our words are going to show our content. It is not easy to control it, it has a power to kill, destroy and produce negative outcomes. "Death and life are in the power of the tongue, and those who love it will eat its fruit." (Proverbs 18:21)

James summarizes the evil effect of our tongue better than I can do it: "My brethren, let not many of you become teachers, knowing that we shall receive stricter judgment. For we all stumble in many things. If anyone does not stumble in word, he is a perfect man, able also to bridle the whole body. Indeed, we put bits in horses' mouths that they may obey us, and we turn their whole body. Look also at ships: although they are so large and are driven by fierce winds, they are turned by a very small rudder wherever the pilot desires. Even so the tongue is a little member and boasts great things. See how great a forest a little fire kindles! And the tongue is a fire, a world of iniquity. The tongue is so set among our members that it defiles the whole body, and sets on fire the course of nature; and it is set on fire by hell. For every kind of beast and bird, of reptile and creature of the sea, is tamed and has been tamed by mankind. But no man can tame the tongue. It is an unruly evil, full of deadly poison. With it we bless our God and Father, and with it we curse men, who have made in the similitude of God. Out of the same mouth proceed blessing and cursing. My brethren, these things ought not to be so. Does a spring send fourth fresh water and bitter from the same opening? Can a fig tree, my brethren, bear olives, or a grapevine bear figs? Thus no spring yields both salt water and fresh." (James 3:1-12)

God has created the world by His spoken word. We do the same. Our words have power on earth and in the spiritual world. We can build up and destroy, bless and curse, encourage and discourage. Spoken words can hurt deeper than a knife. We create reinforcements of reality through our tongue. If we are people of authority, we need to put a guard on our tongue. With our tongue we can break or make our children and the outcome of their lives.

"Let no corrupt word proceed out of your mouth, but what is good for necessary edification, that it may impart grace to the hearers. And do not grieve the Holy Spirit of God, by whom you were sealed for the day of redemption. Let all bitterness, wrath, anger, clamor, and evil speaking be put away from you, with all malice. And be kind to one another, tenderhearted, forgiving one another, even as God in Christ forgave you. But fornication and all uncleanness or covetousness, let it not even be named among you, as is fitting for saints; neither filthiness, nor foolish talking, nor coarse jesting, which are not fitting, but rather giving of thanks." (Ephesians 4:29-32; 5:3, 4)

Our words need to be full of light and bring peace. They need to build and not destroy. They should be free of deceit, hypocrisy and all sort of lying. We should not tear down, destroy nor humiliate. Idle words can be vain words. They are the words that build nothing positive and possibly destroy. When Isaiah had seen the Lord on His thrown, he said the following: "Woe is me, for I am undone! Because I am a man of unclean lips, and I dwell in the midst of a people of unclean lips; for my eyes have seen the King, the Lord of hosts." (Isaiah 6:5)

More scriptures to consider:

- Jeremiah 9:3-9, 23:13-40 Proverbs have many verses concerning the use of tongue and words.
- "For "He who would love life and see good days, let him refrain his tongue from evil, and his lips from speaking deceit. Let him turn away from evil and do good; let him seek peace and pursue it. For the eyes of the LORD are on the righteous, and His ears are open to their prayers; but the face of the LORD is against whose who do evil.""
(1 Peter 3:10-12)
- "For with the heart one believes unto righteousness, and with the mouth confession is made unto salvation." (Romans 10:10)
- "The words of a man's mouth are deep waters, a flowing river, a fountain of wisdom." (Proverbs 18:4 HCSB)
- "Whoever guards his mouth and tongue keeps his soul from troubles." (Proverbs 21:23)
- "Do you see a man hasty in his words? There is more hope for a fool than for him." (Proverbs 29:20)

3. **WORKS:** David has understood the power of the condition of his heart and ability to control his tongue. He has asked the following from the Lord: *"Set a guard, O LORD, over my mouth; keep watch over the door of my lips. Do not incline my heart to any evil thing, to practice wicked works with men who work iniquity; and do not let me eat of their delicacies."* (Psalms 141: 3, 4) When we fail to keep our thoughts and words pure, the wrong actions are sure to follow. If we are mastering our thoughts and words under the Word of God with the help of Holy Spirit, we produce much of the good fruit. Obedience to the Word of God creates an atmosphere around us that will produce positive works which will bring desirable results for the Lord. Our actions spring from our heart, just as it is written: 'you will know them by their fruit.' The fruit of the spirit is going to produce: "love, joy, peace, longsuffering, kindness,

goodness, faithfulness, gentleness, self-control. Against such there is no law. And those who are Christ's have crucified the flesh with its passions and desires." (Galatians 5:22b-24)

The fruit of our unruly sinful flesh is going to produce sins of the flesh: "adultery, fornication, uncleanness, lewdness, idolatry, sorcery, hatred, contentions, jealousies, outbursts of wrath, selfish ambitions, dissensions, heresies, envy, murders, drunkenness, revelries, and the like; of which I tell you beforehand, just as I also told you in time past, that those who practice such things will not inherit the kingdom of God." (Galatians 5:19b-21)

We are to bring the fruit of righteousness and good works daily: "I am the vine, you are the branches. <u>He who abides in Me, and I in him, bears much fruit</u>; for without Me you can do nothing." (John 15:5)

"Brethren, I do not count myself to have apprehended; but one thing I do, <u>forgetting those things which are behind and reaching forward</u> to those things which are ahead, I press toward the goal for the prize of the upward call of God in Christ Jesus." (Philippians 3:13-14) Let us be like Paul '<u>forgetting those things which are behind and reaching forward</u>.' Let us with the Lord's help repent, correct what we can and press on. Let us not allow negative deeds to rob us of our future of positive fruit production for the Lord and our salvation. Paul had done much harm to the body of Christ prior to believing in Him. But he didn't allow it to rob him of the things he could accomplish for Christ. Let us forget and put aside even the good accomplishments we have done, too. For if we dwell on them we may start to boast and may fall into pride. Pride is hateful to the Lord.

"A worthless person, a wicked man, walks with a perverse mouth; he winks with his eyes, he shuffles his feet, he points with his fingers; perversity is in his heart, he devises evil continually, he sows discord. Therefore his calamity shall come suddenly; suddenly he shall be broken without remedy." (Proverbs 6:12-15) What are you sowing? Good or evil? Analyze your own heart, for if you don't, God will: "...God will judge the secrets of men..." (Romans 2:16)

"Rely not on your wealth; say not: "I have the power." Rely not on your strength in following the desires of your heart. Say not: "Who can prevail against me?" For the LORD will exact the punishment. Say not: "I have sinned, yet what has befallen me?" for the LORD bides his time. Of forgiveness be not overconfident, adding sin upon sin. Say not: "Great is his mercy; my many sins he will forgive." For mercy and anger alike are with him; upon the wicked alights his wrath. Delay not your conversion to the LORD, put it not off from day to day; for suddenly his wrath flames forth; at the time of vengeance, you will be destroyed. Rely not upon deceitful wealth, for it will be no help on the day of wrath." (Sirach 5:1-10 NAB) We should not pardon and ignore any sin in our life, for it is of the devil. He is the author of the darkness and all evil. May we do the works of the light, for they are of the Lord. May our works bring the goodness of God where we go and whatever we do or say, regardless of circumstances.

> **CONCLUSION:** Our enemy is looking for ways to do us harm. Our best defense is in obedience to God's Word. It is up to us to build a strong tower around us. From that tower, we can safely work towards protecting and saving our children, husbands, family members and other people. Neglecting the Word of God is going to produce corruption. Our thoughts and words are more important than we think.

➤ **WHAT TO DO: 1.** *PRAY:* 'Dear Holy Spirit, please work in my heart to show me where I need to change and repent. Please, show me how to study the Bible and help me to understand it. Show me the truth, so I and my family can be saved from eternal condemnation. Lord, please give me strength to come to you daily in prayer and Scripture study. Help me to make it a regular habit. Amen.' **2.** Continue with your daily Bible reading and study. Pay attention to the prompting of the Holy Spirit, in this area. Before studying, ask Him to help you understand and apply what you have learned. **3.** Follow other tips from this chapter. **4.** If you find yourself convicted of some of the things being written here, come to the Lord with them. Confess them out loud to Him and repent from them sincerely and ask Him to make you anew and give you strength to stay away from those sins again. Remember, that when you come up short, there is the blood of Jesus which can cleanse you again, just come to Him in repentance and then walk with His help again. **5.** Continue on reading this book.

CHAPTER 3

The Doors of Your House

*"Remind them to be subject to rulers and authorities,
to obey, to be ready for every good work, to
speak evil of no one, to be peaceable, gentle,
showing all humanity to all men."* (Titus 3:1, 2)

I

Every house has at least one door. The spiritual house has six doors. It is up to us to keep those doors shut. For if they are open, the enemy has an opportunity to enter through them. In the last chapter, we discussed one of four pillars as 'authority.' We authorize something all the time by our actions, words and thoughts. But there are other laws of authority which are doors. If we observe them, our doors are closed from the enemy's intrusion. These are: Authority of God, Authority of Parents, Authority of Husband, Authority of Church, Authority of Ordinance of Man, and Authority of Satan. Disobeying and/or disrespecting authority which God has placed can bring huge consequences. Breaking laws of authority can interfere with our prayers and fasting and possibly salvation. We need to correct our situation with laws of authority for our battles to be won and effective.

❖ **Authority of God:** *"For as the rain comes down, and the snow from heaven, and do not return there, but water the earth, and make it bring forth and bud, that it may give seed* *to the sower and bread to the eater, so shall My word be that goes forth from My mouth; it shall not return to Me void, but it shall accomplish what I please, and it shall prosper in the thing for which I sent it."* (Isaiah 55:10, 11)

David sings the following: "For You have magnified Your word above all Your name." (Psalm 138:2c) God Himself has put himself under subject of His own Word. He is not going to break His Word. Jesus has said: "Do not think that I came to destroy the Law or the Prophets. I did not come to destroy but to fulfill. For assuredly, I say to you, till heaven and earth pass away, one jot or one tittle will by no means pass from the law till all is fulfilled. Whoever therefore breaks one of the least of these commandments, and teaches men so, shall be called least in the kingdom of heaven; but whoever does and teaches them, he shall be called great in the kingdom of heaven. For I say to you, that unless your righteousness exceeds the righteousness of the scribes and Pharisees, you will by no means enter the kingdom of heaven." (Matthew 5:17-20)

Satan is the first being who has broken the Most High's authority, due to his pride or pomp, which led him to desire to be like God. This led him to a great fall. "'Your pomp is brought down to Sheol, and the sound of your stringed instruments; the maggot is spread under you, and worms cover you.' How you are fallen from heaven, o Lucifer, son of the morning! How you are cut down to the ground, you who weakened the nations! For you have said in your heart: 'I will ascend into heaven, I will exalt my throne above the stars of God; I will also sit on the mount of the congregation on the farthest sides of the north; I will ascend above the heights of the clouds, I will be like the Most High.' Yet you shall be brought down to Sheol, to the lowest depths of the Pit." (Isaiah 14:11-15) Disrespecting any authority creates problems for the one who dares. Therefore disrespecting the authority of God, His set of authorities and His Word creates unavoidable problems for the disobedient.

Jesus is the very first Being, Who humbled Himself and obeyed the Father and submitted Himself to God's Word and the laws of authority set by the Father: "Who, being in the form of God, did not consider it robbery to be equal with God, but made Himself of no reputation, taking the form of a bondservant, and coming in the likeness of men. And being found in appearance as a man, He humbled Himself and became obedient to the point of death, even the death of the cross. Therefore God also has highly exalted Him and given Him the name which is above every name, that at the name of Jesus every knee should bow, of those in heaven, and of those on earth, and of those under the earth, and that every tongue should confess that Jesus is Lord, to the glory of God the Father." (Philippians 2:6-11)

In return for His obedience and humbleness, Jesus has become the Victor on the white horse, "Now I saw heaven opened, and behold, a white horse. And He who sat on him was called Faithful and True, and in righteousness He judges and makes war. His eyes were like a flame of fire, and on His head were many crowns. He had a name written that no one knew except Himself. He was clothed with a robe dipped in blood, and His name is called <u>The Word of God</u>. And the armies in heaven, clothed in fine linen, white and clean, followed Him on white horses. Now out of His mouth goes a sharp sword, that with it He should strike the nations. And He Himself will rule them with a rod of iron. He Himself treads the winepress of the fierceness and wrath of Almighty God. And He has on His robe and on His thigh a name written: 'King of Kings and Lord of Lords.'" (Revelation 19:11-16)

Now, which side do we want to be on? The side of the one who inherits glory and heaven and all authority? Or the one who is inheriting the lowest depth of hell's pit with maggots, worms and fire? The determination of the destination is up to us. Learn to be humble, for the humble get the grace, the proud always lose it. The humble submit to the Word of God, His will on their lives, and respect His set of authorities. If we want to be sure to be with the Victor on the white horse, we must turn to the Word of God. For this is the name of the Victor. If one is looking for gold, one is going to find it. So if we want to be victors with the Victor, we need to find Him through His Word. God is not partial, He can give us the knowledge of His Word if we truly desire. We must turn only to the pure Word of God, for our society has been indoctrinated with humanism, new age, eastern religion wisdom, secularism, communism, socialism, etc. Unfortunately, these poisons have entered into Christianity. We often can't understand the truth from folly. It is time to scrutinize everything, for time is short and souls are eternal. We can't allow room for folly.

Jesus is the King of kings and Lord of lords. It means that He is above all and in control of all. Being in agreement with such authority is very safe. To go against His authority is very unsafe and unwise. Whenever one disobeys His law and His set authority of any kind, it is going to hurt the disobedient. "Let every soul be subject to the governing authorities. For there is no authority except from God, and the authorities that exist are appointed by God. Therefore whoever resists the authority resists the ordinance of God, and those who resist will bring judgement on themselves." (Romans 13:1, 2)

The only time we are free from obedience to authority, is when we are being asked to do things which are contradictory to our faith like Daniel and his three friends. They refused to disobey the Word of the Most High Authority, God. They refused to obey the set authority of ordinance of man, when it asked them to do things that made them break God's law and obedience to God. They refused to eat the unclean and idol dedicated food, worship idols, and ceasing to pray to the real God.

The disobedience to God in the Garden of Eden has cost all humanity much pain. King Saul's disobedience cost him his kingship: "So Samuel said: "Has the LORD as great delight in burnt offerings and sacrifices, as in obeying the voice of the LORD? Behold, <u>to obey is better than sacrifice</u>, and to heed than the fat of rams. For rebellion is as the sin of witchcraft, and stubbornness is as iniquity and idolatry. Because you have rejected the word of the LORD, He also has rejected you from being king." (1 Samuel 15:22, 23)

Faith in God needs to produce a change in our nature. We need to become His bondservants. We can't believe and still continue in our disobedience. "For as the body without the spirit is dead, so faith without works is dead also." (James 2:26)

II

❖ **Authority of Parents:** *"Honor your father and your mother, that your days may be long upon the land which the LORD your God is giving you."* (Exodus 20:12)

The law of parental authority can heal or curse the land. Malachi prophesied, "Behold, I will send you Elijah the prophet before the coming of the great and dreadful day of the LORD. And he will turn the hearts of the fathers to the children, and the hearts of the children to their fathers, lest I come and strike the earth with a curse." (Malachi 4:5 & 6) Later, John the Baptist came prior to the first visitation of the Lord and prepared the nation for Jesus first coming.

Now, the earth is awaiting the second coming of Jesus or "the day of the Lord" as it is written: "The sun shall be turned into darkness, and the moon into blood, before the coming of the great and awesome day of the LORD." (Joel 2:31) We are in the same need of correcting this law of parental authority as the Jewish nation needed during Jesus time on earth. We need to correct ourselves in this area, too. Obedience in this area heals and takes a curse away.

God is very strong supporter of parental honor, respect and word. This is another law that is important to heed if we are to get victory over our enemy. If we fail to observe and obey God in this area, our prayers are going to be hindered from being answered. Before God answers our prayers, He is going to point to this area and many others. Observing this law is going to heal both parents and children, even marriages and churches. We can't come to the Father unless we obey Him in the law He created for fathers and sons, mothers and daughters. It is time we pick up the wreckage we created as parents and children in order to heal and our prayers to be answered. Children need to come into this authority from one side and parents from the other.

"Children, pay heed to a father's right; do so that you may live for the LORD sets a father in honor over his children; a mother's authority he confirms over her sons. He who honors his father atones for sins; he stores up riches who reveres his mother. He who honors his father is gladdened by children, and when he prays he is heard. He who reveres his father will live a long life; he obeys the LORD who brings comfort to his mother. He who fears LORD honors his father, and serves his parents as rulers. In word and deed honor your father that his blessing may come upon you; for a father's blessing gives a family firm roots, but a mother's curse uproots the growing plant. Glory not in your father's shame, for his shame is no glory to you! His father's honor is a man's glory; disgrace for her children, a mother's shame. My son, take care of your father when he is old; grieve him not as long as he lives. Even is his mind fail, be considered with him; revile him not in the fullness of your strength. For kindness to a father will not be forgotten, it will serve as a sin offering – it will take lasting root. In time of tribulation it will be recalled to your advantage, like warmth upon frost it will melt away your sins. A blasphemer is he who despises his father, accursed of his Creator, he who angers his mother." (Sirach 3:1 -16 NAB)

The above passages says it all. If one wants blessings and the Lord's kindness: obey and respect your parents; do not speak evil or gossip about them; do not forget about them. No 'buts' – if you want blessing and parent(s) are still alive, it is time to ask them forgiveness, respect them, visit them and help them. This is going to bless and heal in return. Asking the Lord to forgive us where we have fallen short in this area, will be a starting process towards healing.

Parents need to change many things, too, so not to hamper their children. Parents need to release their children from the words they have bonded their children with. Also, they need to take responsibility in raising their children in the right way, for God will hold them responsible of their authority.

- **For children:** Most of us are no longer with our parents, but we still need to change many things in order to heal and be blessed and have continuous blessing which passes unto our children, too. Reread and pounder the passage from the book of Sirach. It is impossible to come to the Lord and serve Him without addressing your attitude towards your parents. One needs to repent before the Lord for everything one has done wrong to their father and mother regardless of their parental involvement and abilities (even if one has been abused or abandoned.) We need to repent of our disobedience, dishonor, disrespect and any bad mouthing of our parents, even if our parents are worthy of all our dishonor and evil speaking. We need to forgive our parents for the sake of the Lord and His bonding commandment. If it is hard to forgive, ask God to help you. Make an effort to make any reconciliation with your parents. Ask forgiveness of your parents. Try to get involved with them as much as possible. The older they get the more they need us. Visit them, help them, invite them, call them, write to them, etc. Our goal is to make it right with them because of the Lord and obedience to Him in this commandment. We can't be forgiven unless we forgive! It is very common in our country to find fault with our parents, but restrain yourself, for such practice is a sure way of getting a quick curse into one's life and lives of one's children and into God's disfavor, "Whoever curses his father or his mother, his lamp will be put out in deep darkness. The eye that mocks his father, and scorns obedience to his mother, the ravens of the valley will pick it out, and the young eagles will eat it." (Proverbs 20:20 & 30:17)

- **For parents:** If you are a parent regardless of your children's age, you need to rethink your attitude towards your children. Often we are responsible for their hurt and their turn around. We make many mistakes. If your children are grown – bless them and pray for them. Repent before the Lord for everything you have done wrong. Ask forgiveness if needed from your children. Reconcile with them. Repent for and renounce all the negative things you have spoken into their lives. For often our words have bound them and our prayers can't be effective until we repent of our words and renounce them, and command by the name of Jesus for those words to stop acting in their lives. Learn to respect their individuality and choices. Ask for God's wisdom on how to approach your grown children and how to be useful to them and not the other way around. Be prepared to give good godly advice when the time arises, but refrain from being a constant corrector. If your children are already out of the house, your time has passed, instead pray for them more and continue your relationship with them. Your own changed walk with the Lord and prayer can do more than your nagging words being said at the wrong time and in the wrong way.

Learn to use your tongue in the way it sows blessing into their lives and lives of your grandchildren. Jewish parents are very careful of how they speak to and about their children, for they know the power of parental words. For example, instead of saying 'my son doesn't understand math,' they may say 'my son already knows some math.' When one daughter has stolen a few pounds of gold from her mother, she was cursing whoever has done that. But once she found out that it was her daughter who has done the deed, she has said, "Blessed be my daughter before the God of heaven, for now my daughter has a few pounds of gold!" Our words can curse, bless, break, heal and shape lives of our children, both young and old. Refrain from criticizing them, their spouses, and their children.

"Train up a child in the way he should go, and when he is old he will not depart from it. The rod and rebuke give wisdom, but a child left to himself brings shame to his mother. Correct your son, and he will give you rest; yes, he will give delight to your soul." (Proverbs 22:6 & 29:15, 17) The Bible is full of instruction on how to raise children. The book of Proverbs has many passages with advice. If a child has been trained in the wrong way or not at all, there much work to be done on God's part. Our society is the product of wrong parenting. Parents make many mistakes when raising children. The best approach is to first start with yourself. When we are right with God, we avoid making many mistakes. Children are our clones. They repeat and soak everything from us. Often our weaknesses and sins are repeated by them. Just as we would not let our child play with a chipped lead based paint, we shouldn't give their development to chance either. We need to actively do parenting and bring them up in the way of the Lord.

If you still have children in your home and they are young, be sure to raise them biblically. Help them to be obedient, they need to know that obedience and respect are a great blessing. What kind of example are you giving to your children? Ask God to show you where you make mistakes and how to change. Refrain from using secular books and magazines for your parental wisdom; they usually teach contrary to biblical principles. When you use books for parental wisdom, use common sense, use what works for you and disregard what doesn't.

Remember that each family and each child is different. Use prompting of the Holy Spirit on a day to day basis. Pray daily about God's wisdom and guidance, safety and protection of your children and their salvation. It is possible that you might need to make some changes in the way you parent. Even when your children are teenagers, it is possible to change and undo some parental mistakes. Both toddlers and teenagers are in great need of our parenting. Parenting is a big responsibility before God. One needs to be vigilant in many areas. It is tough to be a parent these days. But you must be brave and strong, for God has put you in such a time as this and entrusted you with your children. I highly recommend you use resources at the end of this book. It is a jungle outside of our house walls. Get some help, it is difficult to do it alone.

God has been very particular about teaching children about His commandments and His ways: "You shall teach them to your children, speaking of them when you sit in your house, when you walk by the way, when you lie down, and when your rise up." (Deuteronomy 11:19) Develop daily devotionals with your children. If your husband

54

doesn't lead the family in devotionals, do it yourself. If he minds it, find time when he can't interfere. It is biblical to teach and lead your children towards God. It is your responsibility to do everything in your power to teach your children about the Lord and worry about your children's salvation. You must be peaceful and respectful towards your husband. If he is an unbeliever and resents everything of God, then you need to be more creative and wise. You need to spend more time on your knees and fasting for the salvation of your husband and children, for wisdom from above in your situation and your husbands softening of the heart towards allowing you to raise your children in the Lord's way.

Many parents have lost their children by not taking them to church and church activities. Also, when they take them to church, they send them to Sunday school. Children must be present with parents at church services and all church activities. By the time they grow up, they are being conditioned to be outside of church walls. When you go to church, be sure your children from birth to eighteen years of age are with you. Take them to all the activities you are personally being involved: Bible studies, funerals, praise and family nights, any volunteering work within the church, etc. They need to feel important, connected and be actively involved in the church alongside of you.

Most importantly, take time to enjoy your children. Love them, respect them, play with them, read to them, etc. Teach them many things. You are going to do them a great favor even when you think they don't listen and don't care. They need to know how to do laundry, clean the house, be neat, how to cook, how to set the table, greet guests, how to be godly husbands and wives, and learn spiritual and daily life wisdom.

III

❖ Authority of Husbands:

- *"Wives, <u>submit</u> to your own husbands, <u>as to the L*ORD*</u>. For the husband is head of the wife, as also Christ is head of the church; and He is the Savior of the body. Therefore, just as the church is subject to Christ, so let the wives be to their own husbands in everything."* (Ephesians 5:22-24) This is the reinforcement of God's law of authority from Genesis 3:16a&c: "To the woman He said: ... Your desire shall be for your husband, and <u>he shall rule over you</u>."

Now, many women do not like and dread this law, especially when husbands are not the kind of leaders they should be and do not return our respect. Nevertheless, we are to obey the law of God. For the commandment not to commit adultery is not for those who are abstinent from this sin but for those who are in this sin or entertaining the possibility of it.

The Lord knows the difficulty of our situation and therefore He tells us through Paul the following words: 'Wives, <u>submit</u> to your own husbands, as <u>to the Lord</u>.' It is very difficult to submit to our fallen Adams, but our submission needs to be to the Lord. All submission to our husbands must be only because of the Lord. If we submit to them out of who they are and not of the Lord, we fall into the possibility of becoming idol worshippers. We are to submit only to the Lord. And all we do in our lives by our thoughts, words, actions, etc. need to be submitted to Him and tested by His Word. Out of our love, respect and submission to the Lord, we must love, respect and submit to our husbands. We must be the wives we need to be to our husbands only because of the Lord. If we want to be obedient to God's authority, we must accept the authority

56

He has placed over us. Being a wife is not easy, it requires much wisdom, patience and dying to self. But with God's Word, prayer, His help and guidance, it is doable. This is an area, which we need to bring daily in our prayers for His wisdom and strength.

Breaking the law of authority in marriage has never been rewarded. Children suffer here the most. There is much pain in our land due to breaking of this law. We all have different natures as do our husbands. We all have unique situations and families. Some may need to work harder than others. If we want blessings, healings and harmony in our families and natures, we need to work on respecting our husbands and giving them opportunity to be what God made them. Men are not perfect, neither are women, for fallen Eves have fallen Adams. Many have different difficult situations in marriages, but they are less likely to be resolved when women disobey the Lord in the law of marriage authority.

I have never seen any blessings in any family and children when a wife has failed to submit to this law. It is not about who and how. Observing this law of authority creates safety for a wife and children in the spiritual realm. When women are repeatedly dishonoring and disobedient, they lose the protection which God gives from observing this law. Observing this law is going to be very crucial in crushing the snake's head. It is also very crucial to keep your authority over the children. It is crucial to have a victory over the snake, this is why you need to observe all authority over you. Thus your fasts and prayers are going to have power and value. If you fail in this law, it is going to be difficult for you to have authority over your children. Also, disobedience in this area is going to interfere with your petitions before God for your children. When a woman respects and obeys her husband as unto the Lord, she has special protection and authority over her children. If a woman breaks this law she loses authority over her children. It becomes very evident when they turn into teenagers.

When a woman is married to an unbeliever, and/or a man unworthy of respect and the only thing she may think to do is run, obedience may be difficult but is of great benefit regardless of the man. I have seen tremendous blessings and turn around where women have stood up to life's trials but have stayed the course in faithfulness in this area. Such women will be called by God blessed. Their children and even their husbands are going to reap the blessed fruit of their obedience. Even when they do not see the fruit of their labor here, they can rest assured, it is not going to be overlooked by the Creator of the women and the Giver of this law.

When women obey this law, even with a hard man there is some order in a family. When a woman is not obeying the law, disorder follows. We have all seen these families in our own circles, where wise women have sustained families, children and husbands because of their obedience to the Lord and perseverance. Others, on the contrary, have had a very good man who went bad due to an unwise woman's disobedience and constant disrespect of her husband. When asked how they've done, they all answer what else could we've done? The difference is one looked through it with eyes of the spirit and the other with eyes of the flesh.

If a woman lives by the spirit she will naturally do the right thing. For living in the spirit wouldn't allow her to bring forth the works of the flesh. When one lives by the flesh, it is a natural reaction to bring forth the things of the flesh. The flesh is selfish, it is incapable of anything outside of selfishness and fallen nature. The woman of the flesh destroys much on her path: husband, children, her parents, church members, churches, and eventually herself. Such a woman is difficult to confront for she slashes out for no reason and has many words and answers to the 'whys' of her misery. Her problems are always someone else's fault. It can be her parents, abusive childhood, husband's inabilities in x-amount of fields, etc. She seem to fail to see herself and what she does on her path.

- *"For man is not from woman, but woman from man. Nor was man created for the woman, but woman for the man."* (1 Corinthians 11:8, 9) We need to remember who has been created for who. We have been created for our men. This is why they marry us. They are not complete without us. We are their helpers. We need to come into the marriage with the expectations that God has placed on us, instead of expectations that we have for ourselves. We need to be useful for them and expect no selfish ambitions in return. When we have less expectations for ourselves, things can get much smoother. "She does him good and not evil all the days of her life." (Proverbs 31:12)

- *"And the LORD God said, 'It is not good that man should be alone; I will make him a helper comparable to him.'"* (Genesis 2:18) We have been created to be helpers. Helpers help. Our men need help to be complete. When we marry them they are far away from perfection, and so are we. The faithfulness and perseverance helps us to develop the character God seeks from us. Helpers need to get help from someone else. Our number one source is God Himself! As women embrace marriage, they will see where and how their help may fit into place. We need to pray for our husbands, daily. Most importantly, we need to be women of God and be who He called us to be. He has given us an ability for many things that we face in marriage. Many of us do not even realize how much we are being helpers on daily basis. Be an encourager and listener, too. Help him to be a leader, stop leading yourself.

Life happens to all of us in different ways. But let's be wise and useful for our husbands for when we help our husbands, we help ourselves and our children. To understand what it means to be a helper takes time. But when we walk with the Lord, we will see it. It is our duty to help him lead, by stepping back and allowing him to be final decision maker on important things. Praying for him in this area is going to allow the process to be less painful.

We should keep our emotions in check with God against the Word of God. If we keep our emotions in check we can give our husbands and others good answers and directions for which we would not need to repent of. Reading the Bible on regular basis and submitting our ways, thoughts, and words to the Word is crucial as a helper. For we influence our husbands and children all the time. If we are out of balance and our emotions gone out of proportions, we may create much negative atmosphere in our home. Regular daily prayer helps to balance many negative emotional outcomes and behaviors. Woman is a thermometer of the home. If it is overheated, things may not go right. If it is balanced, everyone is balanced. Our husbands and children depend on our emotional stability which comes through our daily spiritual health through unbroken relationship with God.

Motherhood and housework is something comes with being a woman. This is not being a helper to a man. This is your role as a women. "She watches over the ways of her household, and does not eat the bread of idleness." (Proverbs 31:27) Men's role is to work and subdue the land or earn the bread: "In the sweat of your face you shall eat bread." (Genesis 3:19a)

- *"The <u>wife does not have authority over her own body, but the husband does</u>. And likewise the husband does not have authority over his own body, but the wife does. <u>Do not deprive one another</u> except with consent for a time, that you may give yourselves to fasting and prayer; and come together again so that <u>Satan does not tempt you because of your lack of self-control</u>."* (1 Corinthians 7:4, 5) Ladies, feed your husbands sexually. He has been designed differently, he loves you and this is the reason why he married you in a first place. Do your duty, feed that guy of yours.

- *"... Let the wife see that she respects her husband."* (Ephesians 5:33b) For man sees love through respect. Women often fail in this area when they get too familiar with their husbands. Their mouth does the most disrespect. Learn to speak to your husband and hold your tongue where needed. Do not allow your words to rush out of your mouth, prior to your consideration of what their end result is going to be. Women seem to know how to speak and respect other people in the office and work, but not always their husbands. The Bible says the following: "She opens her mouth with wisdom, and on her tongue is the law of kindness." (Proverbs 31:26) Women often do much damage with their words. Both Peter and Paul teach women to bite their tongue. It may sound like a harsh punishment, but on contrary it is a tip for peace and harmony in marriage. Women simply forget that their husbands are not their girlfriends and their mothers. Not everything needs to be said and silence is actually their best friend. Women may be overly concerned with their looks, but instead they need to be more concerned with their attitudes, conduct and words. "Wives, likewise, be submissive to your own husbands, that even if some do not obey the word, they, without a word, may be won by the conduct of their wives, when they observe your chaste conduct accompanied by fear. Do not let your adornment be merely outward – arranging the hair, wearing gold, or putting on fine apparel – rather let it be the hidden person of the heart, <u>with the incorruptible beauty of a gentle and quiet spirit, which is very precious in the sight of God</u>." (1 Peter 3:1-4)

- *"A good name is to be chosen rather than great riches, loving favor rather than silver and gold."* (Proverbs 22:1) Do not gossip about your husband. His bad reputation is not going to help you. Whatever happens between the two of you should be left with both of you and God. (Yes, not even a little bit.) Only positive information should ever come out of your lips about him, even to your mom. "Her husband is known in the gates, when he sits among the elders of the land." (Proverbs 31:23) Your mouth can break or make his reputation, therefore yours and of your children. Never speak evil of your husband to your children. Your children do not need to get even the slightest idea from your words and attitude that their father is not worthy of respect.

- *"Let a woman learn in silence with all submission. And I do not permit a woman to teach or to have authority over a man, but to be in silence. For Adam was formed first, then Eve. And Adam was not deceived, but the woman being deceived, fell into transgression."* (1 Timothy 2:11-14) Russian translation of these verses refers to a husband and a wife. Here we have a secret of underlying protection. When a woman respectfully approaches her husband and allows him to lead and make final decisions, and when she respects his lead in devotions, it protects her from making another mistake like what happened in the Garden of Eden.

There shouldn't be a stubborn demand on always being her way in decision making and leading devotions according to her understanding. Refrain from correcting him on theological themes: discussions – yes, teaching and constant correction – no. If you think his theology is not scriptural, it is time to seriously bring it to the Lord, daily.

With feminism in force, modern women have forgotten to allow men to lead both spiritually and in decision making. This in turn, can be hampering our prayers, blessings and protection by God from false teaching, demonic attacks against the women and possible attachment of evil spirit(s). These spirits can work through them in destruction of them, their husbands, their children and even churches. The best example in the Bible is Jessabelle and Ahab. This woman has done much damage to the nation of Israel, has been a subject of the failed king and husband, and eventually her own destruction and that of her children.

- *"The wise woman builds her house, but the foolish pulls it down with her hands."* (Proverbs 14:1) Many women make many mistakes and continue on. Many marriages could have been much happier and could have been saved if the women had been careful in their conduct. Some men are indeed difficult, and in such situations one needs much patience and strength from the Lord. But often women's behavior makes or breaks marriages and families. "Charm is deceitful and beauty is passing, but a woman who fears the Lord, she shall be praised. Give her of the fruit of her hands, and let her own works praise her in the gates." (Proverbs 31:30, 31) The works of our hands are going to determine the happiness of our husbands and our children. We must take our responsibility, love and pray for our husbands, and let the Lord do the work on our husbands. When God is going to ask us, we need to be ready to answer to Him for our actions and not for actions of our husbands.

IV

❖ **Authority of Church:** *"And He Himself gave some to be apostles, some prophets, some evangelists, and some pastors and teachers, for the equipping of the saints for the work of ministry, for the edifying of the body of Christ."* (Ephesians 4:11, 12) From this verse we see that God is again in charge of another authority and over the elders and positions in the church. Disrespect of this authority is again going to be against God's perfect design of authority and structure for the church. Here again, we must be very careful in what we do, for this is the establishment of which, God Himself is in charge.

"But Peter said, "Ananias, why has Satan filled your heart to lie to the Holy Spirit and keep back part of the price of the land for yourself? While it remained, was it not your own? And after it was sold, was it not in your own control? Why have you conceived this thing in your heart? You have not lied to men but to God." Then Ananias, hearing these words, fell down and breathed his last. So great fear came upon all those who heard these things." (Acts 5:3-5) Ananias has died for the sin of hypocrisy. He didn't even say one word!

What is our initiative for everything we do in the church? Are we seeking our own gain and agenda? We must seek the benefit of Christ and His body? It is very dangerous to speak evil of the people in charge in the church. It is not right to gossip even about lay members. One needs to be careful in the church for there dwells the Holy Spirit. Also, church is made up of people in whom dwells the Holy Spirit. "Do you not know that you are the temple of God and that the Spirit of God dwells in you? If anyone defiles the temple of God, God will destroy him. For the temple of God is holy, which temple you are." (1 Corinthians 3:16, 17) We must honor the authority and every member in the church.

Apostle Paul states to us even further: "The cup of blessing which we bless, is it not the communion of the blood of Christ? The bread which we break, is it not the communion of the body of Christ? For we, though many, are one bread and one body; for we all partake of that one bread. Therefore whoever eats this bread or drinks this cup of the Lord in an unworthy manner will be guilty of the body and blood of the Lord. But let a man examine himself, and so let him eat of the bread and drink of the cup. For he who eats and drinks in an unworthy manner eats and drinks judgment to himself, not discerning the Lord's body. For this reason many are weak and sick among you, and many sleep. For if we would judge ourselves, we would not be judged." (1 Corinthians 10:16, 17 & 11:27-31) We are to analyze ourselves in the light of Scripture and teachings of Christ in everything, including all pertaining to the church and Jesus' requirements and laws within the church. For many become weak, sick and sleep or die ("sleep" refers to death.)

Breaking the rules and authority of the church is dangerous. For one is dealing with God, for Jesus has the authority over the church. Also, he has made men, who are husbands and they are heads of wives. It makes clear sense that He makes men above women in church, too. They should be in charge or in leadership positions within the church. "Wives, submit to your own husbands, as to the Lord. For the husband is head of the wife, as also Christ head of the church; and He is the Savior of the body. Therefore, just as the church is subject to Christ, so let the wives be to their own husbands in everything." (Ephesians 5:22-24) Saying this, it doesn't mean that every man has authority over every woman. What it means is that God places men in a higher position over women in His church; and that every man is in authority of his own wife. No other man should take authority over someone else's wife. But men have higher placement in the leadership in the church setting. In the Old Testament only male Levites have been allowed to do all services in and around the temple. It is very clear that is how God wants it now, too. The abundance of men in the church brings no need for women to hold pastoral positions.

"Let your women keep silent in the churches, for they are not permitted to speak; but they are to be submissive, as the law also says. And if they want to learn something, let them ask their own husbands at home; for it is shameful for women to speak in church." (1 Corinthians 14:34, 35) These are very harsh words indeed. I don't like them any better than you do. But, these are words for our own protection. Women can speak where it is permissible and with due respect. All women should be cautious for their own sake to not break God's placement of authority and take liberty in going above man's authority in the church. For when a woman goes outside of this protection, she opens the door for evil spirit(s) to work through her in her disobedience and do much harm within the church. The most common spirit is the spirit of Jezebel. This spirit works through a woman to manipulate and destroy church members and churches. Such a woman usually already has trampled the law of authority of her husband and lives in unrepented sin (usually sexual related). Jesus said, "Nevertheless I have a few things against you, because you allow that woman Jezebel, who calls herself a prophetess, to teach and seduce My servants to commit sexual immorality and eat things sacrificed to idols." (Revelation 2:20) Now, this doesn't mean, that every woman that teaches is bad and sinful and brings destruction. She should not teach men within the church, unless it is allowed by the church authority under strict discretion by the set authority and members of the church. Woman should not rush into pastoral positions. She can be very vulnerable without the protection that is only given to a man for this position.

Women can and should be useful and fruitful within the church and outside the church. "There is neither Jew nor Greek, there is neither slave nor free, there is neither male nor female; for you are all one in Christ Jesus." (Galatians 3:28) There is much work to be done by both men and women, for the harvest is in need of laborers. "For as we have many members in one body, but all the members do not have the same function, so we, being many, are one body in Christ, and individually members of one another. Having then gifts differing according to the grace that is given to us, let us use them: if prophecy, let us prophesy in proportion to our faith; or ministry, let us use it in our ministering; he who teaches, in teaching; he who exhorts, in exhortation; he who gives, with liberality; he who leads, with diligence; he who shows mercy, with cheerfulness. (Romans 12:4-8)

Our churches are going to begin to heal when our men will stand up boldly for the truth in our churches. We need to pray for them, for pastors, and other elders in our churches. We need to allow God to come in our midst, and for this reason prayer and obedience to His set ordinance in church is very important. Churches are in a huge need of God, a very huge need. Let's allow our men to be the Levites as they used to be.

V

❖ **Authority of Ordinance of Man:** "Therefore submit yourselves to every <u>ordinance of man for the Lord's sake</u>, whether to the king as supreme, or to governors, as to those who are sent by him for the punishment of evildoers and for the praise of those who do good. For this is the will of God, that by doing good you may put to silence the ignorance of foolish men – as free, yet not using liberty as a cloak for vice, but as bondservants of God. Honor all people. Love the brotherhood. Fear God. Honor the king. Servants, be submissive to your masters with all fear, not only to the good and gentle, but also to the harsh. For this is commendable, if because of conscience toward God one endures grief, suffering wrongfully." (1 Peter 2:13-19) God's established authorities need to be obeyed and respected within the limits of the Scripture: God is the highest authority of everything and everyone. He dictates and sets rules and laws. He has established all authority: "Then Pilate said to Him, "Are You not speaking to me? Do You not know that I have power to crucify You, and power to release You?" Jesus answered, "You could have no power at all against Me unless it had been given you from above. Therefore the one who delivered Me to you has the greater sin."" (John19:10, 11) Authority has power. God is the one with power and He gives it to everyone as He wishes.

"At the beginning of the reign of Zedekiah the son of Josiah, king of Judah, this word came to Jeremiah from the LORD: "This is what the LORD said to me: Make fetters and yoke bars for yourself and put them on your neck. Send word to the king of Edom, the king of Moab, the king of the Ammonites, the king of Tyre, and the king of Sidon through messengers who are coming to Zedekiah king of Judah in Jerusalem. Command them to go to their masters, saying: This is what the LORD of Hosts, the God of Israel, says: This is what you must say to your masters: By My great strength and outstretched arm, I made the earth, and the people, and animals on the face of the earth. I give it to anyone I please. So now I have placed all these lands under the authority of My servant Nebuchadnezzar, king of Babylon. I have even given him the wild animals to serve him. All nations will serve him, his son and his grandson until the time for his own land comes, and then many nations and great kings will enslave him. "As for the nation and kingdom that does not serve Nebuchadnezzar the king of Babylon and does not place its neck under the yoke of the king of Babylon, that nation I will punish by sword, famine, and plague" – this is the LORD's declaration – "until through him I have destroyed it.""" (Jeremiah 27:1-8 HCSB)

From the above passage we see that political power is from the Lord. God even calls the ruler Nebuchadnezzar as His servant. He is obviously a gentile and has been an idol worshipper, but God has placed him in the land politically in order to accomplish certain things. Apostle Peter tells us to 'submit ourselves to every ordinance of man for the Lord's sake.' Also, Paul teaches us to pray for them, "First of all, then, I urge that petitions, prayers, intercessions, and thanksgivings be made for everyone, for kings and all those who are in authority, so that we may lead a tranquil and quiet life in all godliness and dignity. This is good, and it pleases God our Savior, who wants everyone to be saved and to come to the knowledge of the truth. For there is one God and one mediator between God and man, a man, Christ Jesus, who gave Himself – a ransom for all, a testimony at the proper time." (1 Timothy 2:1-6 HCSB)

Both Peter and Jude speak of not 'rejecting authority and speak evil of dignitaries.' "Likewise also these dreamers defile the flesh, reject authority, and speak evil of dignitaries. Yet Michael the archangel, in contending with the devil, when he disputed about the body of Moses, dared not bring against him a reviling accusation, but said, "The Lord rebuke you!" But these speak evil of whatever they do not know; and whatever they know naturally, like brute beasts, in these things they corrupt themselves. These are grumblers, complainers, walking according to their own lusts; and they mouth great swelling words, flattering people to gain advantage." (Jude 8-10, 16) Thus we can come to the following conclusions:

1. All ordinances of man is from the Lord: that includes our husbands, parents, pastors, teachers, bosses, presidents, senators, governors, city mayors, judges, police, etc.
2. We are not to dishonor nor disrespect them or speak evil about them. We are not to disobey them, unless they are asking us to do contrary to the Word of God.
3. We are to pray for them and bless them for in doing so we improve our own quality of life and receive protection.

Jesus has shown us an example through His life of submission to God the Father, the Word of God and all authority placed by God. He further tells us the following: "Come to Me, all you who labor and are heavy laden, and I will give you rest. Take My yoke upon you and learn from Me, for I am gentle and lowly in heart, and you will find rest for your souls. For My yoke is easy and My burden is light." (Matthew 11:28:30) One is to learn from Him how to be humble before God, die to self and be a servant. "But he who is greatest among you shall be your servant. And whoever exalts himself will be humbled, and he who humbles himself will be exalted." (Matthew 23:11, 12)

Such an approach brings healing. This world is fallen. It is in sin. Sin brings much misery into our lives. The only way one can get healing and be set free of many behaviors which may harm others is only by submitting to God and His Word. Healing comes slowly and over time in faithfulness to God's Word and relationship with the Healer. Humbleness, forgiveness and taking responsibility for ones' own actions, words and thoughts are steps toward recovery of one person at a time which in turn can heal the rest around them. Selfishness is creating problems, for it points fingers, blames others, makes excuses, hurts others and refuses to compromise unless it benefits only self.

If we live by the flesh we create a misery in our circles, to ourselves and jeopardize our salvation. For the flesh is contrary to the spirit. Regardless of our life circumstances, we need to submit to our Lord, His authority and His Word. Carnal Christians are difficult to deal with. They find excuses for not being the way they should be by finding reasons for their problems. They never seem to find fault with themselves, but see many faults with others. The Bible has a whole list of their sinful attributes, which are addressed to Christians of our time: "But know this, that in the last days perilous times will come: for men will be lovers of themselves, lovers of money, boasters, proud, blasphemers, disobedient to parents, unthankful, unholy, unloving, unforgiving, slanderers, without self-control, brutal, despisers of good, traitors, headstrong, haughty, lovers of pleasure rather than lovers of God, having a form of godliness but denying its power. And from such people turn away!" (2 Timothy 3:1-5)

Lovers of themselves are self-pleasers. They worship only selves. It is their pride that they pursue. Pride always manifests itself in disobedience and disrespect to authorities. There is no feeling of guilt when one justifies the prideful gratification of self. It is our fallen flesh. It always finds fault with others and can't seem to submit to anything. This is exactly what Jesus died for, to help us submit our flesh under grace and His law of love, humbleness and servanthood to God first and then to others: "For all the law is fulfilled in one word, even in this: "You shall love your neighbor as yourself. Beloved, let us love one another, for love is of God; and everyone who loves is born of God and knows God. He who does not love does not know God, for God is love." (Galatians 5:14 & 1 John 4:7, 8)

"Love suffers long and is kind; love does not envy; love does not parade itself, is not puffed up; does not behave rudely, does not seek its own, is not provoked, thinks no evil; doesn't rejoice in iniquity, but rejoice in the truth; bears all things, believes all things, hopes all things, endures all things." (1 Corinthians 13: 4-7) 'Love doesn't seek its own' – modern day wisdom is to seek its own. If you find such teaching, run from it. When pride is being fed, it is going to fall. When humbleness grows, it grows into healing self and others.

Whenever one thinks to break any authority for what one makes claim to as 'God's calling,' one needs to really have good scriptural grounds and remember that 'to obey is better than sacrifice.' "So Samuel said: "Has the LORD as great delight in burnt offerings and sacrifices, as in obeying the voice of the LORD? Behold, to obey is better than sacrifice, and to heed than the fat of rams. For rebellion is as the sin of witchcraft, and stubbornness is as iniquity and idolatry. Because you have rejected the word of the LORD, He also has rejected you from being king." (1 Samuel 15:22, 23)

VI

❖ **Authority of Satan:** From Genesis 3:15 *"I will put enmities between thee and the woman, and thy seed and her seed: she shall crush thy head, and thou shalt lie in wait for her heel."* (Douay-Rheims Bible) From this verse, we see that God has allowed the enmity between the woman and her seed, or human offspring after her and especial in female gender. Then we find in the following verse that there are set authorities in the heavenly places: "For we do not wrestle against flesh and blood, but against principalities, against powers, against the rulers of the darkness of this age, against spiritual hosts of wickedness in the heavenly places. Therefore take up the whole armor of God, that you may be able to withstand in the evil day, and having done all, to stand." (Ephesians 6:12, 13) We find more evidence of spiritual realm in book of Revelation and Daniel 10:13, 20, 21. We see that these dark authorities are subject to God as of Job chapter 1. Let's cover 'authority of satan' in next chapter.

➤ **CONCLUSION:** All authority is from God. Obeying, respecting and praying for authority is a benefit, protection and blessing. We can disobey authority only on scriptural ground, but never disrespect or speak evil and bad mouth.

➤ **WHAT TO DO:** *1.* Repentance with confession before God always sets a new record and starts a page in our life anew. If you find yourself guilty in this area, repent and confess. Then keep your doors closed by being right with the authority for the Lord's sake and obedience of His Word. *2.* Start praying for authority that touches your life. *3.* Pray: 'Lord, please help me to respect and be obedient to You, Your Word, and other authorities in my life. Thank You for creating authority for my own protection and blessing.' *4.* Continue to study the Word of God with the help of the Holy Spirit. For the purity of milk and food of God, avoid any man-made studies. *5.* Tell others about this book, so they can benefit from this, too.

CHAPTER 4

The Roof of Your House

I

"Finally, draw your strength from the Lord and from his mighty power. Put on the armor of God so that you may be able to stand firm against the tactics of the devil. For our struggle is not with flesh and blood but with the principalities, with the powers, with the world rulers of this present darkness, with the evil spirits in the heavens. Therefore, put on the armor of God, that you may be able to resist on the evil day and, having done everything, to hold your ground. So stand fast with your loins girded in truth, clothed with righteousness as a breastplate, and your feet shod in readiness for the gospel of peace. In all circumstances, hold faith as a shield, to quench all the flaming arrows of the evil one. And take the helmet of salvation and the sword of the Spirit, which is the word of God. With all prayer and supplication, pray at every opportunity in the Spirit. To that end, be watchful with all perseverance and supplication for all the holy ones." (Ephesians 6:10-19 NAB)

From the above passage, we see that Christians are in a warfare. Also, in Genesis 3:15 *"I will put enmities between thee and the woman, and thy seed and her seed: she shall crush thy head, and thou shalt lie in wait for her heel,"* we see that

74

snake leads an enmity or warfare with a woman and her seed. When Adam and Eve have willingly disobeyed, they opened the door to the devil.

It is evident from the Scriptures that we are in a war with satan. He is having an enmity with us and working against us. Why? The true answer we can find in the Bible, again. Apostle Peter tells us that the gospel which is preached to us is desirable by angels: "…preached the gospel to you by the Holy Spirit sent from heaven. Angels desire to look into these things." (1 Peter 1:12b HCSB) Angels are serving spirits which are made by God to serve us. We are sons and daughters of God through Christ. Even though angels have more strength than us, they are in a lesser position than us. For there is nothing more glorious than to be sons and daughters of God and therefore brothers and sisters of Jesus. God's angels who are already with God and in heaven want to take our place. The fallen angels do not have such opportunity for salvation as us, therefore they lead a hateful warfare against our privilege and position in Christ.

The fallen angels forever have lost heaven and opportunity for salvation and the ability to see God's approval. The fallen angels, or servants of satan and darkness, know that their time is coming to an end, and their final judgment is the everlasting fire, maggots and worms. They know that we are going to the place, where they can never come. Therefore, they are actively seeking any opportunity to tear us from our course to heaven. Their goal is to prevent us from heaven and take us with them to hell for eternity.

They have been successful with many. Many are being deceived daily and will fall into hell. The biggest deception is still at work. It hasn't changed from the Garden of Eden. The snake told Eve that she would not die. Now we are told that we are guaranteed our salvation and that nothing can separate us from Christ's love. Nothing can separate us from love of Jesus, but sin can separate us from Him and heaven, for "nothing unclean, and no one who practices abomination and lying, shall ever come into it..." (Revelation 21:27a NASB)

If our salvation is guaranteed, there is no point to warfare or any point of guarding anything. Jesus, Paul, Peter, John, James and Jude have warned us of the dangers. We are told in Philippians to "work out our salvation with fear and trembling." Peter reminds us to "Be sober, be vigilant; because your adversary the devil walks about like a roaring lion, seeking whom he may devour." (1 Peter 5:8) Paul gives us instructions in Ephesians 6:10- 29 on how to protect our salvation and our spiritual building through armor of God. *The armor of God is **the roof of our spiritual house.***

II

The Bible gives us very clear instructions on how to be victorious and overcome the evil one:

"Therefore submit to God. Resist the devil and he will flee from you. Draw near to God and He will draw near to you. Cleanse your hands, you sinners; and purify your hearts, you double-minded." (James 4:7, 8) Let's analyze how we can overcome the 'roaring lion' by breaking this passage in three parts:

I. **Submit to God, draw near to God and He will draw near to you:**

    According to the Ephesians passage, we are to *"draw our strength from the Lord and from his mighty power."* Jesus has said, "Abide in Me, and I in you. As the branch cannot bear fruit of itself, unless it abides in the vine, neither can you, unless you abide in Me. I am the vine, you are the branches. He who abides in Me, and I in him, bears much fruit; <u>for without Me you can do nothing</u>." (John 15:4, 5) The same applies to every aspect of our life. We cannot protect ourselves from the evil one, for we can't even breath without God. The Lord enables us to breath, assimilate food, think and function physically. He also enables us to believe, produce fruit for Him, pray, understand His Word and have protection. He is our source for everything. All the gifts we have are of Him, we shouldn't boast or take any credit for it. Wisdom comes from Him alone, for He is Wisdom.

Salvation and our ability to produce good works come from Him, too. "For by grace you have been saved through faith, and that not of yourselves; it is the gift of God, not of works, lest anyone should boast. For we are His workmanship, created in Christ Jesus for good works, which God prepared beforehand that we should walk in them." (Ephesians 2:8-10)

We are to fear and be concerned only of God's opinion, "And do not fear those who kill the body but cannot kill the soul. But rather fear Him who is able to destroy both soul and body in hell." (Matthew 10:28) *If we abide in Him,* we need to rest assured that God is still in control of all things, because of Jesus victory on Calvary. His goal is to bring us to heaven and help us along the way. He knows that we are fallen and in the flesh on the earth's hostile environment. He is not going to allow us to be tempted beyond what we are able. "No temptation has overtaken you except such as common to man; but God is faithful, who will not allow you to be tempted beyond what you are able, but with the temptation will also make the way of escape, that you may be able to bear it." (1 Corinthians 10:13)

We are to grow closer to Him, daily. The closer we are to Him, the more secure and protected we will be to Him. Matter of fact, He is to consume our thoughts, for we are to think of the things above not of the things of this earthy life. For whatever pulls us stronger may overpower us. Earth is passing, God and heaven are everlasting. Therefore, we are to be more concerned about spiritual things than physical.

God gives us the armor of God, 'that we may be able to resist on the evil day, having done everything, to hold our ground.' "Therefore, put on the armor of God, that you may be able to resist on the evil day and, having done everything, to hold your ground. So stand fast with your loins girded in truth, clothed with righteousness as a breastplate, and your feet shod in readiness for the gospel of peace. In all circumstances, hold faith as a shield, to quench all the flaming arrows of the evil one. And take the helmet of salvation and the sword of the Spirit, which is the word of God. With all prayer and supplication, pray at every opportunity in the Spirit. To that end, be watchful with all perseverance and supplication for all the holy ones." (Ephesians 6:13-19 NAB) The armor of God is the roof of our house. It is useless to build any structure if the roof is not part of the plan. The leaking roof can undermind any good building. God enables us, but it is up to us to use the armor. For we need to do our part, so He can do His part for us:

- ***Stand fast with your loins girded in truth:*** We need to know the truth, and only the truth. For if what we base our building on is not truth, it is going to collapse. It may even cost us and others the loss of salvation. One needs to get into the Word to find the truth. There is no substitution. There is no 'fast food' in learning and eating the truth – the Word of God. Many have paid a dear price for lack of discipline in the study of the Word of God. They have taken an instant 'knowledge shake' from someone else. The most popular books and studies can be our worst enemies. There is a best seller out there by a most popular writer. Pick it up and start reading, it is the Holy Bible and specially tailored for all souls who are serious about the Author and the way to Him. It is pure and suitable spiritual food.

- **Clothed with righteousness as a breastplate:** The breastplate protects us from being hurt in the vulnerable places like a heart, a liver, etc. It is extremely important. For if one gets hurt in the heart or other organs, it can be fatal. The enemies job to take with him as many as possible. We are to put righteousness as a breastplate, it shouldn't be taken lightly. "For sin shall not be master over you, for you are not under law, but under grace. What then? Shall we sin because we are not under law but under grace? <u>May it never be</u>!" (Romans 6:14, 15 NASB) Matter of fact, here's what Apostle Peter tells to those who think that grace is for the justification of any sin: "Therefore, dear friends, while you wait for these things, make every effort to be found in peace without spot or blemish before Him. Also, regard the patience of our Lord as an opportunity for salvation, just as our dear brother Paul, according to the wisdom given to him, has written to you. He speaks about these things in all his letters, in which there are some matters that are hard to understand. <u>The untaught and unstable twist them to their own destruction, as they also do with the rest of the Scriptures.</u> Therefore, dear friends, since you have been forewarned, be on your guard, so that you are not led away by the error of the immoral and fall from your own stability." (2nd Peter 3:14-17 HCSB) And so, Scriptures have been taken and twisted to one's own agenda of easy living and happy Christian living of no regards to sin.

God hates sin, how can He justify it? Pride and disobedience are not going to enter heaven. For He has cast both of these from heaven and the earthly paradise. Has God changed because of Christ? No, for it is written that He never does. So, let's return to the solid understanding of Scriptures. Grace is to help us grow into His Son's likeness. It is also there because no one is righteous and therefore no one deserves to go to heaven to be in the presence of the most Holy God. But through Jesus, God forgives. Every sin needs to be confessed and repented of verbally and in the inner heart. Therefore, one needs to run away from sin and walk in repentance daily for we sin much, and Jesus blood needs to wash us daily. For "If we say that we have no sin, we deceive ourselves, and the truth is not in us. If we confess our sins, He is faithful and just to forgive us our sins and to cleanse us from all unrighteousness. If we say that we have not sinned, we make Him a liar, and His word is not in us." (1 John 1:8-10) We are to "work out our own salvation with fear and trembling." (Philippians 2:12b) There is no middle ground, one either makes it to heaven or hell. There is zero room for religious play.

If one values her soul, than perhaps one should consider those words of Paul: ""Now the works of the flesh are evident, which are: adultery, fornication (Matthew 5:27, 28), uncleanness, lewdness, idolatry (Colossians 3:5, 1 Samuel 15:23), sorcery (1 Samuel 15:23), hatred, contentions, jealousies, outbursts of wrath, selfish ambitions, dissensions, heresies, envy, murders (1 John 3:15), drunkenness, revelries, and the like; of which I tell you beforehand, just as I also told you in the past, that those who practice such things will not inherit the kingdom of God. But the fruit of the Spirit is love, joy, peace, longsuffering, kindness, goodness, faithfulness, gentleness, self-control. Against such there is no law. And those who are in Christ's have crucified the flesh with its passions and desires. If we live in the Spirit, let us also walk in the Spirit." (Galatians 5:19-24) Please, take a dictionary and look up the meaning of these words. This is the Word of God, if it says so, it is so. I put in parenthesis a few scriptures for more study and explanation of some of these descriptions or listed sins.

I don't know about you, but when I started to grow in the Lord, and my relationship has grown stronger and closer with the Lord, I have been convicted of so many things where I am wrong, that I dare not call myself righteous. I repent daily of my fallen nature. The longer I am a Christian the dearer Jesus sacrifice and blood becomes to me. I am a sinner, hopeless sinner. My thoughts, desires, words, and works come short of His glory and righteousness. When I face His Face I face Him only because of His Dear Son's blood. I am unworthy for this Holy Being to shed His blood for me. But He did, and He called it grace, for when I am worthless, His blood makes me clean and pure. Mind you, I do not under humble myself, nor do I boast, I always wonder how others want to make to heaven without the need for His blood? They commit sin without a blink and continue on like it is O.K. Well, it is not O.K. Grace is not a ticket for sin, but for a realization that one is a hopeless sinner. "For if we sin willfully after we have received the knowledge of the truth, there no longer remains a sacrifice for sins, but a certain fearful expectation of judgment, and fiery indignation which will devour the adversaries. Anyone who has rejected Moses' law dies without mercy on the testimony of two or three witnesses. Of how much worse punishment, do you suppose, will he be thought worthy who has trampled the Son of God underfoot, counted the blood of the covenant by which he was sanctified a common thing, and insulted the Spirit of grace? For we know Him who said, "Vengeance is Mine, I will repay," says the Lord. And again, "The Lord will judge His people." It is a fearful thing to fall into the hands of the living God." (Hebrews 10:26-31)

Therefore, 'the breastplate of righteousness' is to run away from sin and walk in constant repentance before the Lord. "I can do all things through Christ who strengthens me." (Philippians 4:13) That is including staying away from all sin and overcoming even the stubborn ones.

- ***Your feet shod in readiness for the gospel of peace:*** Our gospel is peace, why then wherever we go we quarrel? Jesus has said, "Blessed are the peacemakers, for they shall be called sons of God." (Matthew 5:9) Apostle Paul sums up 'gospel of peace' this way: "Bless those who persecute you; bless and do not curse. Rejoice with those who rejoice, and weep with those who weep. Be of the same mind toward one another. Do not set your mind on high things, but associate with the humble. Do not be wise in your own opinion. Repay no one evil for evil. Have regard for good things in the sight of all men. If it is possible, as much as depends on you, live peaceable with all men. Beloved, do not avenge yourselves, but rather give place to wrath; for it is written, "Vengeance is Mine, I will repay," says the Lord. Therefore "If your enemy is hungry, feed Him; if he is thirsty, give him a drink; for in so doing you will heap coals of fire on his head." Do not be overcome by evil, but overcome evil with good." (Romans 12:14-21)

We are going to bring to the Kingdom of Heaven more fruit if we do just this. Often our witness doesn't justify our conduct. We need to walk the walk before we talk.

Jesus has said, "You have heard that it was said to those of old, 'You shall not murder, and whoever murders will be in danger of the judgement.' But I say to you that whoever is angry with his brother without a cause shall be in danger of the judgement. And whoever says to his brother, 'Raca!' shall be in danger of the council. But whoever says, 'You fool!' shall be in danger of hell fire. Therefore if you bring your gift to the altar, and there remember that your brother has something against you, leave your gift there before the altar, and go your way. <u>First be reconciled to your brother, and then come and offer your gift. Agree with your adversary quickly, while you are on the way with him, lest your adversary deliver you to the judge, the judge hand you over to the officer, and you be thrown into prison.</u> Assuredly, I say to you, you will by no means get out of there till you have paid the last penny." (Matthew 5:21-26)

Having shoes of 'the gospel of peace' is important for us, for if we are not careful with our relationship affairs, we are in danger of our prayers not being heard and possible condemnation. Therefore, be a peacemaker and make things right with those to whom you have done wrong. If the other party is guilty, asked God how it can be reconciled. The goal is to reconcile and make things right, so no knots can prevent us from worshipping the Maker and interfere with our salvation.

It is better to tolerate some things instead of proving a point at the expense of peace and give into things that can be sinful. "Why not rather put up with injustice? Why not rather be cheated? Instead, you act unjustly and cheat – and this to brothers! Do you not know that the unjust will not inherit God's kingdom? (1 Corinthians 6:7b-9a HCSB)

The 'gospel of peace' can be summed into this: "And just as you want men to do to you, you also do to them likewise. For all the law is fulfilled in one word, even in this: "You shall love your neighbor as yourself."" (Luke 6:31 & Galatians 5:14)

III

- ***In all circumstances, hold faith as a shield, to quench all the flaming arrows of the evil one:*** We are to have faith in all circumstances, for doing so, no flaming arrows of the evil one are going to be effective. The enemy's goal is to make us doubt God, undermine our faith and cause us to walk away from God. There are many different circumstances in life, for it is life, but we mustn't allow those circumstances to influence our faith into disbelief of God. "My brethren, count it all joy when you fall into various trials, knowing that the testing of your faith produces patience. But let patience have its perfect work, that you may be perfect and complete, lacking nothing." (James 1:2-4)

Trials are a benefit to us. They allow us to grow stronger in the Lord, test our faith and our building. It is like growing a tree. All weather is beneficial for the growth: rain, snow, sunshine, cold, wind, etc. If a tree from a protected environment is to be planted in an unprotected area, it may get sick and even wither and die. The same is with us, God allows different atmospheres while making us strong and useful.

In our trials, no matter how harsh they are, we need to remember the following truths:

a) *God is in control:* "For by Him all things were created that are in heaven and that are on earth, visible and invisible, whether thrones or dominions or principalities or powers. All things were created through Him and for Him. And He is before all things, and in Him all things consist. And He is the head of the body, the church, who is the beginning, the firstborn from the dead, that in all things He may have the preeminence." (Colossians 1:16-18) Also, read Ephesians 1:19-23.

b) *He is faithful to help us through:* "No temptation has overtaken you except such as is common to man; but God is faithful, who will not allow you to be tempted beyond what you are able, but with the temptation will also make the way of escape, that you may be able to bear it." (1 Corinthians 10:13)

c) *He still remembers and knows us:* "Are not five sparrows sold for two copper coins? And not one of them is forgotten before God. But the very hairs of your head are all numbered. Do not fear therefore; you are of more value than many sparrows." (Luke 12:6)

d) *He still loves us:* "For God so loved the world that He gave His only begotten Son, that whoever believes in Him should not perish but have everlasting life." (John 3:16)

e) ***It is of benefit to us:*** "…we also glory in tribulations, knowing that tribulation produces perseverance; and perseverance, character; and character, hope. Now hope does not disappoint, because the love of God has been poured out in our hearts by the Holy Spirit who was given to us." (Romans 5:3b-5) Also, read James 1:2-4.

f) ***God exists:*** His Son died for us and He is the only way to the Father. Not only Scripture speaks about it, but history proves it, too. "Jesus said to him, "I am the way, the truth, and the life. No one comes to the Father except through Me. I am the door. If anyone enters by Me, he will be saved, and will go in and out and find pasture." (John 14:6 & 10:9)

"Blessed is a man who endures trials, because when he passes the test he will receive the crown of life that He has promised to those who love Him. No one undergoing a trial should say, "I am being tempted by God." For God is not tempted by evil, and He Himself doesn't tempt anyone. But each person is tempted when he is drawn away and enticed by his own evil desires. Then after the desire has conceived, it gives birth to sin, and when sin is fully grown, it gives birth to death." (James 1:12-15 HCSB)

When life gets tough, we need to bring to our mind different Biblical heroes: Joseph, Daniel and his three friends, Elijah, Jeremiah, Paul, and first Christians, and draw even closer to the Lord.

- ***Take the helmet of salvation:*** Being hit on the head can be fatal, so one needs to have a helmet for protection. We are to put on 'the helmet of salvation.' Claiming and believing that one is saved may not be necessarily so. Our belief must be grounded on the Scripture, for "Not everyone who says to Me, 'Lord, Lord,' shall enter the kingdom of heaven, but he who does the will of My Father in heaven." (Matthew 7:21) Jesus has given us the proverb of a wedding, which shows us that many are called but not many are chosen. Now, are you among the called or chosen? God is not partial, He has died for the whole humanity. Now, what determines between the two? It is those who love Him and who do the will of the Father. If we truly love God, we would do the things He asks us to do and hate the things He hates. He loves holiness and people, He hates disobedience and sin.

When one puts on the helmet of salvation, one must obey the Word. Many claim positive promises without any basis for them. Our salvation is conditional, His conditions are all over the New Testament writings. Let's look just at a few:

- "And he who does not take his cross and follow after Me is not worthy of Me." (Matthew 10:38)
- "You search the Scriptures, for in them you think you have eternal life." (John 5:39a)
- "Most assuredly, I say to you, if anyone keeps My word he shall never see death." (John 8:51)
- "If you abide in My word, you are My disciples indeed. And you shall know the truth, and the truth shall make you free." (John 8:31b-32)
- "He who has an ear, let him hear what the Spirit says to the churches. To him who overcomes I will give to eat from the tree of life, which is in the midst of the Paradise of God." (Revelation 2:7)

It is up to us to analyze the building of our spiritual house and whether or not we are building on the right foundation. It is up to us to analyze where we stand with God, correct where we come short and carry out our salvation on daily basis. This is going to be our 'helmet of salvation.' We are to "work out our own salvation with fear and trembling, being watchful to this end with all perseverance and supplication…" (Philippians 2:12b & Ephesians 6:18b)

If one thinks that first prayer has guaranteed the place in heaven, one is deceived. It is nowhere in Scriptures. If only this prayer saves, then the Bible would be very slim. God has made it a point to write to us in many different ways repeatedly of His ways for a reason, "Enter by the narrow gate; for wide is the gate and broad is the way that leads to destruction, and there are many who go in by it. Because narrow is the gate and difficult is the way which leads to life, and there are few who find it." (Matthew 7:13, 14)

"'Father,' he said, 'then I beg you to send him to my father's house – because I have five brothers – to warn them, so they won't also come to this place of torment.' "But Abraham said, 'They have Moses and the prophets; they should listen to them.' "'No, father Abraham,' he said, 'But if someone from the dead goes to them, they will repent.' "But he told him, 'If they don't listen to Moses and the prophets, <u>they will not be persuaded</u> if someone rises from the dead.'" (Luke 16:27-31 HCSB)

And so it is true for our day. The Lord has taken a few individuals to hell and back. Some have died and by mercy of God have been returned. They all testify that people who thought were Christians are in hell. People simply do not believe and consider it non-scriptural that God would send any Christians to hell. Those people are burdened with sins and enjoy them, and have no desire to give them up. They use Scripture to justify themselves and lull themselves into a deception and a spiritual sleep. Those people reject all the testimonials about hell and also any warnings in the Scriptures.

I know one pastor who has been in hell in a section for those who are awaiting the judgment day. (It is not a purgatory, no one is being purged of any sins, there. Once in hell, you are in hell.) According to him, that place is in a form of a cup the size larger than our planet earth. It is full of Christians who are waiting for the judgment day. Their bodies decompose and stink like the rest of people in hell. They scream hysterically, beg for mercy and confess their sins. No one cares there anymore. They no longer embarrassed by their sins, but unfortunately it is too late. According to the pastor, there is no guarantee for hope of forgiveness or justification at the judgment day.

- ***The sword of the Spirit, which is the Word of God:*** The knowledge of the Word of God is crucial in our salvation, spiritual house building, and having on the entire armor of God. No matter what we do, we deal with the Word of God. God has created everything through His Word. He continues to hold everything by His Word. He is going to judge every human being by His Word. We use it as a spiritual sword in order to cut away anything that is not based on His Word, which determines all the truth. "But He answered and said, "It is written, 'Man shall not live by bread alone, but by every word that proceeds from the mouth of God.'" (Matthew 4:4) We are to learn it, eat it, drink it, study it, read it, meditate on it, we are to write it on our hearts. We submit to God by obeying to His Word. His Word is our life. His Word is Jesus.

"For the word of God is living and powerful, and sharper than any two-edged sword, piercing even to the division of soul and spirit, and of joints and marrow, and is a discerner of the thoughts and intents of the heart. And there is no creature hidden from His sight, but all things are naked and open to the eyes of Him to whom we must give account." (Hebrew 4:12, 13)

IV

- ***"With all prayer and supplication, pray at every opportunity in the Spirit. To that end, be watchful with all perseverance and supplication for all the holy ones."***

NKJV has it this way: "praying always with all prayer and supplication in the Spirit, being watchful to this end with all perseverance and supplication for all the saints." Let's us break this verse into several sections for better understanding:

- *We are to 'pray always with all prayer and supplication and at every opportunity':* Prayer is our communication with God, "Be anxious for nothing, but in everything by prayer and supplication, with thanksgiving, let your request be made known to God; and the peace of God, which surpasses all understanding, will guard your hearts and minds through Christ Jesus." (Philippians 4:6, 7) In our prayers, we can tell Him our worries and problems, "casting all your care upon Him, for He cares for you." (1 Peter 5:7) All men of God have prayed. Daniel was willing to be eaten by lions over ever missing His time with God in his daily prayer. In prayer we let our needs be known, we praise and worship Him, converse with Him, and repent of our sins.

  Prayer is our tool of defense and offense. Through prayer, we let our desires and petitions be known. We are to pray particularly over our many spiritual needs and protection from the enemy. Here are some things to pray for: for God to finish our salvation, for God to guard us of any evil and satan's schemes, wisdom in every aspect of our life (at work, at church, in marriage, in child rearing, etc.), knowledge and understanding of His Word and will, for the future, for our husbands and children, and many things that we are concerned about.

  The Word of God is our spiritual food. Praying in the Spirit is our spiritual water. Regular prayer is our spiritual oxygen. Without oxygen a human body cannot live. It takes just a few minutes or even seconds for the physical body to die without oxygen. The body can sustain without water intake for several days and without food up to forty days. But without oxygen it has very short life span. This is why we are to be in the Word of God, praying in Spirit, and praying always and without ceasing, daily. "Pray without ceasing. Do not quench the Spirit." (1 Thessalonians 5:17, 19)

All three components are very important for our building of the house and to be victorious. But prayer is something, when not done on a regular basis can weaken our defenses. Through prayer we preserver and get much needed support and give authority to God to intercede on our behalf. In the last days, it is especially important, for time is nearing the end and being always ready is very important. Prayer gives us the empowerment to continue on.

If the Word of God is a spiritual sword, it becomes even more powerful when it is used in prayer. If prayer by itself is the strong weapon, then when we pray with the use of the Word, it becomes an explosion. The combination of the two makes the kingdom of darkness tremble and stand back. The combination of these two can overturn many obstacles and move mountains. Use it to pray for yourself and others. When I started to pray with the Word of God, things have changed greatly for the better. I and those I have prayed for have grown spiritually in faith and strength.

- *We are to 'pray for all saints':* In the next verse Paul writes "and for me, that utterance may be given to me, that I may open my mouth boldly to make known the mystery of the gospel, for which I am an ambassador in chains; that in it I may speak boldly, as I ought to speak." (Ephesians 6:19, 20) If Paul needed prayers, so do we. We are to pray for ourselves and others, for we are all in need of grace and support. We are family and one body, we should support each other. Praying for other saints actually helps us heal spiritually and even physically "...Pray for one another, that you may be healed." (James 5:16b) Isn't it amazing! If one cares for one's own body, one can get healed. The same applies to our spiritual body, the church of Christ! We need each other! Praying for each other builds immunity within the body of Christ! We are being attacked by evil forces daily. We need immunity as much as we can get.

We are to pray for our pastors, other church leadership, and for individual members, especially those who need our prayers the most and those who have no one else to pray for them. Also, consider adopting in prayer any Christian organization, gospel preacher, and/or missionary. They are the ones that need our prayers the most. They actively work to expand the kingdom of heaven, therefore they experience much opposition from the kingdom of darkness.

We need to pray daily for the persecuted body of Christ. They are in great need of our daily praying support. We are not only should, we are obligated to pray for them: "And if one member suffers, all the members suffer with it; or if one member is honored, all the members rejoice with it. Now you are the body of Christ, and members individually." (1 Corinthians 12:26, 27) We are all aware of severe persecution of Christians all over the world and especially in Middle East. Their human rights are violated beyond imagination. They lose their livelihood, homes, jobs, wives, children, husbands, parents and their own lives. Many women and children are raped and sold into sexual slavery. Many are tortured and then killed. There are many orphaned children because of that, too. I personally believe that ignoring their sorrows is a sin against Christ. If we all unite daily for them in prayer, the kingdom of darkness is going to have limited power over them. Oh, how much God needs us to pray in this area, for He needs our prayers to rescue and help many. The spiritual battles can be overcome and won with much prayer and fasting. The persecuted church members need our prayers for support.

Here is a sample prayer, but feel free to create your own: *"Lord, be the wall of fire all around persecuted Christians around the world, especially in Muslim believing countries and North Korea, and be glorified in their midst. Help them to be strong, patient and faithful. Show them mercy and Your divine protection and intervention. Ease their suffering and give them endurance. Have mercy on their children and their souls. Let their persecutors come to repentance, for our Savior desires all men to be saved."*

Remember one thing – prayer warriors receive greater rewards in heaven, for without prayer even the best preacher is weak and of little use. Prayer is the only tool that enables the Holy Spirit to move within our midst and advance for the kingdom of God. It enables preaching and any other work fruitful and more glorious!

• *We are to 'pray at every opportunity in the Spirit':* In the book of Hebrew it says, "...Christ, who through the eternal Spirit offered Himself without spot to God..." (Hebrew 9:14b) Even Jesus, Son of God, needed the Holy Spirit to offer without blemish Himself to God. How much more than we are in need of the Holy Spirit. Before being raised to the Father, Jesus commanded His disciples to stay in Jerusalem and wait for the Promise of His Father saying, "you have heard from Me; for John truly baptized with water, but you shall be baptized with the Holy Spirit not many days from now. But you shall receive power when the Holy Spirit has come upon you; and you shall be witnesses to Me in Jerusalem, and in all Judea and

Samaria, and to the end of the earth." (Acts 1:4c-5, 8) Here are other words of Jesus about the Holy Spirit:

○ "But the Helper, the Holy Spirit, whom the Father will send in My name, He will teach you all things, and bring to your remembrance all things that I said to you." (John 14:26)

○ "However, when He, the Spirit of truth, has come, He will guide you into all truth; for He will not speak on His own authority, but whatever He hears He will speak; and He will tell you things to come. He will glorify Me, for He will take of what is Mine and declare it to you." (John 16:13, 14)

Holy Spirit*: *1. The Helper – His job is to help on our journey to heaven. *2.* The Spirit of truth – guides us into all truth. *3.* The Teacher – teaches us all things we need to know. *4.* The Reminder – brings to us remembrance of all things that Jesus has said to the disciples. *5.* Under authority of God – whatever He hears He will speak to us. *6.* The Foreteller of the future – He tells us of things to come. *7.* The Glorifier of Christ – He glorifies Jesus, for He takes of what is His and declares it to us. *8.* Enables with power – we shall receive power when the Holy Spirit comes upon us. *9.* Enables us to be witnesses of Jesus.

The starting point of receiving Him has been recorded: "When the Day of Pentecost had fully come, they were all with one accord in one place. And suddenly there came a sound from heaven, as of a rushing mighty wind, and it filled the whole house where they were sitting. Then there appeared to them divided tongues, as of fire, and one sat upon each of them. And they were all filled with the Holy Spirit and <u>began to speak with other tongues, as the Spirit gave them utterance</u>." (Acts 2:1-4) This is exactly what Paul is talking about of how to pray in the Spirit. This is one way and there is no other way.

It is up to every Christian, regardless of their denomination, to ask God to baptize them with Holy Spirit. In order to have our whole complete package of the protection from the evil one and wear the whole armor of God, we need to pray in the Spirit as Apostle Paul teaches. "So I say to you, ask, and it will be given to you; seek, and you will find; knock, and it will be opened to you. For everyone who asks receives, and he who seeks finds, and to him who knocks it will be opened. If a son asks for bread from any father among you, will he give him a stone? Or if he asks for a fish, will he give him a serpent instead of a fish? Or if he asks for an egg, will he offer him a scorpion? If you then, being evil, know how to give good gifts to your children, how much more will your heavenly Father give the Holy Spirit to those who ask Him!" (Luke 11:9-13)

If you are already baptized with the Holy Spirit with the sign of speaking in other tongues, great! Continue praying in them. The Spirit is going to work within you in many things and pray for you where you need it most. The more you pray the better for you, your spiritual growth, and your protection and power. "Likewise the Spirit also helps in our weaknesses. For we do not know what we should pray as we ought, but the Spirit Himself makes intercession for us with groanings which cannot be uttered." (Romans 8:26) The Spirit's job is to help us and pray for us. He often prays ahead of time and also makes things easier in the hard and difficult times we face, but we must pray in the Spirit (tongues) in order for it to take place.

If you are not baptized, you can start asking God daily in prayer to baptize you. God is going to make this baptism happen. It happens in many ways to different people.

Before you start the petition before God about baptism of the Holy Spirit, you need to analyze your entire life through the lenses of Scripture. Repent and confess all your sins. Close the sixth door (which follows right after this) by confession, repentance and renouncing any involvement with it (including any sexual sins), even if you were involved in those things prior to your conversion. The Holy Spirit only enters into a pure heart, which has completely and honestly repented and renounced any involvement with things that God hates. (Note: if those things are not taken care of, another spirit which is not of God can take liberty to enter. But not to be afraid, those things shouldn't happen, for God doesn't allow those things to people who love Him and honestly serve Him with the pure heart.)

"But an hour is coming, and now is, when the true worshipers shall worship the Father in spirit and truth; for such people the Father seeks to be His worshipers. God is spirit, and those who worship Him must worship in spirit and truth." (John 4:23, 24 NASB) The Word of God is spiritual, we build spiritual house, we are to live by the Spirit, worship by the spirit; it makes sense to seek God in prayer about being baptized by His Spirit to make things much easier for us to serve our God spiritually. "'Not by might nor by power, but by My Spirit,' says the Lord of hosts." (Zechariah 4:6b) It is so much easier when we 'receive the gift of the Holy Spirit.' (Acts 2:38c)

It is absolutely 100% scriptural to be baptized by the Holy Spirit with the sign of speaking in tongues. The book of Acts talks primarily about such baptism as the only way. Then in the whole New Testament we find one hundred percent proof of such concept. Before His departure to heaven, Jesus said the following: "And these signs will follow those who believe: In My name they will cast out demons; <u>they will speak with new tongues</u>; they will take up serpents; and if they drink anything deadly, it will by no means hurt them; they will lay hands on the sick, and they will recover." (Mark 16:17, 18) Perhaps, we lack miraculous works today, because we forgot about their Author, the Holy Spirit, and the way to receive Him.

➢ ***Conclusion:*** Satan is actively seeking to cause us harm and interfere with our salvation. Therefore, we should not slumber and do what we can to protect our place in heaven. The closer we are to the Lord, the safer we are. Daily prayer and Bible study enable us to accomplish much more than just accumulating knowledge. God has given us the gift of the Holy Spirit to help, teach, and protect. It is up to us to use this gift to God's potential.

➢ ***What to do: 1.*** Pray: 'Lord, please put the whole armor of God on me. Please, show me where I am lacking Your protection. Give me wisdom and ability to change where changes are due. Amen.' ***2.*** Analyze yourself, do you have the armor of God on? ***3.*** Correct with the Lords help what needs to be corrected. ***4.*** If you find yourself short on many things, take it to the Lord in prayer with repentance.

V

II. Resist the devil and he will flee from you:

We can resist the snake. Eve could resist the snake. She could wait out the time when God comes to interact with Him and ask the Lord about the snake and his cunning way. Instead she decided that to be like God would be better and fell for the trick.

Which way do we allow the snake to short cut our freedom and salvation? What can be better than God and heaven? What do you love the most, God or that something in your life? Paul teaches us: "nor give place to the devil" (Ephesians 4:27), in another words do not open him a door or a window. Just like Eve had opened a place for the devil, we can open one, too. Satan is looking for any opportunity to get into the house: any crack, any open window or door, even if it is just a little opening. For once he is there, he can open all the doors and windows, take off the roof, and undermine a foundation.

- *Cracks:* Cracks in the building of a foundation, walls and roof can be fixed by going back into the Word, prayer, repentance, sometimes fasting, and submission to God by drawing to Him.
- *Doors:* Doors can be closed by repenting, submitting and respecting God and His authority in our lives.
- *Windows:* Windows are our sins. Ours sins allow *'the law of sin'* to have dominion over us which is death: "But each one is tempted when he is drawn away by his own desires and enticed. Then, when desire has conceived, it gives birth to sin; and sin, when it is full-grown, brings forth death. He who sins is of the devil, for the devil has sinned from the beginning. For this purpose the Son of God was manifested, that He might destroy the works of the devil. Whoever has been born of God does not sin, for His seed remains in him; and he cannot sin, because he has been born of God. In this the children of God and the children of the devil are manifest: Whoever does not practice righteousness is not of God, nor is he who does not love his brother." (James 1:14, 15 & I John 3:8-10) Repentance is a must and we must walk away from all sin.

❖ ***Sixth Door or Authority of Satan:*** *"And the person who turns to mediums and familiar spirits, to prostitute himself with them, I will set My face against that person and cut* *him off from his people."* (Leviticus 20:6) People open this door usually due to their ignorance. Once opened, it is hard to close. It leads to almost complete submission to the enemy instead of God. If this door is open, only the mercy of God and/or someone else's prayers can sustain this person from destruction and eternal condemnation. Usually, even God can't interfere for the person who voluntary has opened the door. For we can't cross the enemy's territory without him claiming his right and authority over us.

1. *Rejecting, denying and turning away from God.* This is a person's way to show that one has no need for God and the other option is a different master. It is either servanthood to God or satan. There is no neutral road. If one thinks he or she is their own master, one is in big denial. It is therefore dangerous to deny Christ verbally when being pressured into rejecting the Christian faith. "Therefore whoever confesses Me before men, him I will also confess before My Father who is in heaven. But whoever denies Me before men, him I will also deny before My Father who is in heaven." (Matthew 10:32, 33)

2. *Voluntarily serving satan by personal decision and possible ritual:* This is extremely dangerous, and with little chance of return or escape. Witches, warlocks, people who sold themselves for favors, etc. are some examples.

3. *Participation whether knowingly or unknowingly in things of satan:* "For You have abandoned Your people, the house of Jacob, because they are full of divination from the East and of fortune-tellers like the Philistines. They are in league with foreigners." (Isaiah 2:6 HCSB)

    a. Reading books on witchcraft (including Harry Potter, Narnia, Lord of Rings, about all sorts of dragons, vampires, magic, etc.) "Does a spring send forth fresh water and bitter from the same opening?" (James 3:11) How can witchcraft become Christian, we can't take witchcraft to illustrate Biblical points. It is an abomination to God.

b. Watching the above mentioned movies and cartoons.

c. Participation and reading eastern wisdom, their religious books, yoga, alpha, new age, marshal arts, Christian Science, most meditations and meditational music.

d. Using homeopathy, acupuncture and many other eastern medical practices. Be very careful of things that are claimed to be natural. The enemy likes to mingle himself into natural healing. As they say, "If in doubt, leave it out."

e. Bringing into the home and keeping the above mentioned materials.

f. Bringing into the house idols, and other objects that are used in false religion rituals and witchcraft.

g. Celebrating Halloween and participation in anything to do with it, like visiting the stores and horror stands or attractions.

h. Participating in any way in witchcraft of all form, horoscope reading, fortune telling, palm reading, card foretelling and playing (since the common playing cards are used in witchcraft, they are witchcraft item and one should not play them), etc.

i. Listening to satanic meditation music, hard rock and heavy metal. Those things are produced and inspired by satan. The makers have testified of it themselves. There is no Christian rock or metal music, it is a deception.

Note: I have met Christians who have been actively justifying participation in yoga, Halloween, playing cards and all the above mentioned things as being non harmful. They reason that they do nothing with the devil and they really don't mean to serve the author. It only takes once to cross the line for the enemy to make a claim over one's life and one's soul. Eve didn't mean to sell all humanity to satan, horrific evil, suffering and hell. The Bible says the following: "Adulterers and adulteresses! Do you not know that friendship with the world is enmity with God? Whoever therefore wants to be a friend of the world makes himself an enemy of God." (James 4:4) Here we have more than friendship with the world, we have friendship with the devil. One doesn't only become enemy to God, one becomes friend to satan and allows him to become his master.

4. *Reading and studying the depths of satan and angels:* "Now to you I say, and to the rest in Thyatira, as many as do not have this doctrine, who have not <u>known the depths of Satan,</u> as they say, I will put on you no other burden." (Revelation 2:24) Why search for something that is not in the Bible? The Bible has given us everything we need to know. Anything beyond that is dangerous and has cost many dearly. "What is too sublime for you, seek not, into things beyond your strength search not. <u>What is committed to you, attend to; for what is hidden is not your concern</u>. With what is too much for you meddle not, when shown things beyond human understanding. Their own opinion has misled many, and false reasoning unbalanced their judgment." (Sirach 3:20-23 NAB) It has become extremely popular to study the spiritual world for the sake of knowing which spirit deals with us and how to command it to leave. Such study is actually forbidden by God and dangerous, for we are to study things of God and not of satan. Studying any witchcraft, spiritism and about angels, even if it claims Christian is very dangerous. It has effected many people mentally and even turned into demon possession. Avoid all these materials no matter how Christian they may claim to be. Biblical warfare which we talk about in this book is the safest way one can go.

Paul writes the following: "Let no one disqualify you, insisting on ascetic practices and the worship of angels, claiming access to a visionary realm and inflated without cause by his fleshly mind." (Colossians 2:18 HCSB)

5. *Unrestricted commanding and binding:* Unrestricted commanding and binding of things or spirits one does not know and or has authority over is extremely dangerous. It is wise to avoid doing any such things. Have you seen Jesus bonding and commending in the way many do today? Many have been taking upon themselves more than they can handle or have been allowed. Nowhere in the Bible is there a mention of such activities as we are practicing today, even by Jesus and His apostles. Our spiritual battles are won through obedience of the Word, being close to the Lord, staying away from sin, praying with our words and in the Spirit and fasting. We are allowed to cast out demons out of people, providing all the necessary requirements are met. We also can command demons out of our personal homes if we find any activity and their presence, but with no particular name naming. We do not need to command any problems or spirits to leave. When we do this, we are actually calling on ourselves more problems and taking direct contact with the spirits we have no match of strength. Study the Bible, there are plenty of instructions; walk closer to the Lord for His divine protection and wisdom. Tell Him about the problem, only when direction is given, one can act. Be patient, in many cases one is being tested or going through a trial. Once the time of testing is over, the situation is going to clear by itself.

6. *Evil speaking:* "However angels, who are greater in might and power, do not bring a slanderous charge against them before the Lord." (2 Peter 2:11 HCSB) Just as with any authority we should not speak evil of our spiritual enemy and his servants, nor talk or pray to them.

7. *Sexual immorality:* Sexual immorality always comes along with idol worship, false religion, and dealing with anything where the snake is the author. Falling into practicing it and viewing porn can never come unpunished. Adultery,

fornication and pornography have been the doors of demon possession in many Christians.

➢ ***Conclusion:*** All of the above things may create mental problems, demon possession and grounds for devil to contend for one's soul before God and win.

➢ ***What to do: 1.*** Sit down with a piece of paper and pen and look through your life. Write down all the incidences of the above things. Repent and confess all of them, and renounce any involvement with them. Ask Jesus to cleanse you of all of it and to cover you with His blood. If you think you need the help of a pastor, use it. ***2.*** Collect and <u>burn</u> all the items you have found that are not appropriate in your home. Repent for having them in your possessing and bringing them in your home. Renounce any involvement with them. (Throwing away is not an option, burning and renouncing any involvement with the materials is going to set you free.)

VI

III. Cleans your hands, you sinners; and purify your hearts, you double-minded:

Wow, this is very clear. It is calling us to repent of sins and to turn away from them. "But your iniquities have separated you from your God; and your sins have hidden His face from you, so that He will not hear. For your hands are defiled with blood, and your fingers with iniquity; your lips have spoken lies, your tongue has muttered perversity. No one calls for justice, nor does any plead for truth. They trust in empty words and speak lies; they conceive evil and bring forth iniquity." (Isaiah 59:2-4) Sin is hateful to God. How can we justify it in our lives then?

The life with sin compromising leads to double-mindness: "… a double-minded man, unstable in all his ways." (James 1:8) We either serve Him wholeheartedly or not. We all have ups and downs, but it is dangerous to drift away from the Lord or snooze. As we have this saying, "You snooze – you lose." We need to make a decision to serve God and not both masters. One can't serve God and do what He hates – sin. Jesus came to set us free from sin how can we live in it and justify it. Also, we can't serve two masters. We are going to serve that which we love the most. If our god and our love is of this earth, the corruption is unavoidable.

"No one can serve two masters; for either he will hate the one and love the other, or else he will be loyal to the one and despise the other. You cannot serve God and mammon." (Matthew 6:24) Money is such a god that it consumes us and adds other sins to it. "But those who desire to be rich fall into temptation and a snare, and into many foolish and harmful lusts which drown men in destruction and perdition. For the love of money is a root of all kinds of evil, for which some have strayed from the faith in their greediness, and pierced themselves through with many sorrows." (1 Timothy 6:9, 10) Jesus has said the following, "Take heed and beware of covetousness, for one's life does not consist in the abundance of the things he possesses." (Luke 12:15b) For "Now godliness with contentment is great gain. For we brought nothing into this world, and it is certain we can carry nothing out. And having food and clothing, with these we shall be content." (1 Timothy 6:6-8)

We find Jesus addressing Martha, "Martha, Martha, you are worried and troubled about many things. But one thing is needed, and Mary has chosen that good part, which will not

<u>be taken away from her.</u>"" (Luke 10:41b, 42) Jesus sees deeper than we do: "Man does not see what the LORD sees, for man sees what is visible, but the LORD sees the heart." (1st Samuel 16:7c HCSB) This is why Martha's extra care has been disapproved by Jesus for "… Martha was distracted by her many tasks." (Luke 10:40a HCSB) In other words, she has been consumed beyond what is needed for the moment. A simple meal should have been in place for such a time as this. She was too busy for a deeper realization that the son of God was visiting her and that she needed to take all the opportunity to learn from Him, visit with Him and build relationship with Him.

We can understand Jesus plea to Martha in the following passage: "So don't worry, saying, 'What will we eat?' or 'What will we drink?' or 'What will we wear?' For the idolaters eagerly seek all these things, and your heavenly Father knows that you need them. <u>But seek first the kingdom of God and His righteousness, and all these things will be provided for you.</u> Therefore don't worry about tomorrow, because tomorrow will worry about itself. Each day has enough trouble of its own." (Matthew 6:31-34 HCSB)

The whole story with Martha and Mary is teaching us the importance of priorities. Things that are pertaining to eternity, our salvation and spiritual matters should be placed first. "So if you have been raised with the Messiah, seek what is above, where the Messiah is, seated at the right hand of God. <u>Set your minds on what is above, not on what is on the earth.</u> For you have died, and your life is hidden with the Messiah in God." (Colossians 3:1-3 HCSB) All other things can fall into their place. Jesus promises to meet our needs after our eternal needs are met. Placing our earthly matters first can cost us too dearly; we might miss the blessings our Father has prepared for us and lose our eternal souls.

Jesus has given us a parable of ten virgins. "Now five of them were wise, and five were foolish. Those who were foolish took their lamps and <u>took no oil</u> with them, but the <u>wise took oil</u> in their vessels with their lamps. But while the bridegroom was delayed, they all slumbered and slept. And at midnight a cry was heard: 'Behold, the bridegroom is coming; go out to meet him!' Then all those virgins arose and trimmed their lamps. And the foolish said to the wise, '<u>Give us some of your oil, for our lamps are going out</u>.' But the wise answered, saying, 'No, lest there should not be enough for us and you; but go rather to those who sell, and buy for yourselves. And while they went to buy, the bridegroom came, and those who were ready went in with him to the wedding; and the door was shut." (Matthew 25:2-10)

'Give us some of your oil, for our lamps are going out' – this is a request for something impossible to give and share. For the oil is prepared beforehand. The oil is a state of readiness and strength that comes through many days of studying the Scripture, checking yourself against the Word of God, walking in obedience to the Word of God and His will, being filled in the Spirit, filling up the cup by praying and fasting ahead of time for the upcoming events, and continuously growing in faith, strength and relationship with the Lord. The oil is a continuous daily walk with the Lord.

Double-minded people serve themselves and other objects, but holding on to God for they want to go to heaven. The very things that hold them are going to prevent them from heaven, for it is idolatry in God's eyes. If we want heaven, we need to hold on to Christ and deny ourselves, for God seeks those who are obsessed with Him alone. He calls such people 'bondservants.' In Russian, it really interprets as 'slaves.'

> **CONCLUSION:** We should take our own salvation seriously. We even need to put on the whole armor of God to keep from losing our salvation. We need to actively pursue God, for the closer we are to Him the safer we are from temptation and the enemy. It can all be summed up into the very first and most important commandment: *"Jesus answered him, "The first of all the commandments is: 'Hear, O Israel, the LORD our God, the LORD is one. And you shall love the LORD your God with all your heart, with all your soul, with all your mind, and with all your strength.' This is the first commandment.""* (Mark 12:29, 30)

> **WHAT TO DO:** Instructions are given in the text. Continue with the daily Bible study, prayer, and reading of this book.

CHAPTER 5

Blow the Trumpet in Zion

I

"And the LORD spoke to Moses, saying, "Speak to the children of Israel, and say to them: 'The feasts of the LORD, which you shall proclaim to be holy convocations, these are My feasts.'" (Leviticus 23:1, 2)

𝒯he feasts of the Lord are important for us to pay attention to and even celebrate them in the light of the New Testament, for they are signifying events that are directly related to us. These seven feasts are represented as a seven lamp stand, "...there is a lampstand of solid gold with a bowl on top of it, and on the stand seven lamps with seven pipes to the seven lamps. Two olive trees are by it, one at the right of the bowl and the other at its left." (Zachariah 4:2b-4)

Jesus is the main stand on whom this stand is setting. Through Him and by the God's Spirit these feasts are going to come to pass: "For behold, I am bringing forth My Servant the BRANCH." & "'Not by might nor by power, but by My Spirit,' says the LORD of hosts." (Zach. 3:8c & 4:6b) 'The two olive trees' represent the two witnesses from Revelation chapter 11: "These are the two olive trees and the two lampstands standing before the God of the earth." (Rev. 11:4) These witnesses are coming very soon, at the time or right before the 'sign of woman' in Revelation chapter 12.

Jesus has completed the very first of three feasts in one Jewish spring month and within one week. These are three ***spring feasts***:

1. ***Passover*** (Lev. 23:5): "The next day John saw Jesus coming toward him, and said, "Behold! The Lamb of God who takes away the sin of the world!" (John 1:29) Jesus' blood and sacrifice has spilled for forgiveness of our sins, taking off our curses and healing of body and spirit. We eat and drink His body and blood to remember His suffering and what He has done for us. We no longer need to bring animal sacrifices to wash away our sins. Instead, when we repent, His blood washes our sins.

2. ***Feast of Unleavened Bread*** (Lev 23:6-8): "And Jesus said to them, "I am the bread of life. He who comes to Me shall never hunger, and he who believes in Me shall never thirst." (John 6:35)
   "Do you not know that a little leaven leavens the whole lump? Therefore purge out the old leaven, that you may be a new lump, since you truly are unleavened. For indeed Christ, our Passover, was sacrificed for us. Therefore let us keep the feast, not with old leaven, nor with the leaven of malice and wickedness, but with the unleavened bread of sincerity and truth." (1 Cor. 5:6b-8) We are to be sin free. We are to run away from sin. When we fall into sin because of our human fallen nature, we have the blood of Jesus to cleanse us if we repent and confess our sins (read 1 John 1:8-10).

3. ***Feast of Firstfruits*** (Lev 23:10): "But now Christ is risen from the dead, and has become the firstfruits of those who have fallen asleep." (1 Corinthians 15:20) We need to put Jesus and serving God first in our lives.

Summer feast is completed through the promise by Jesus of the baptism of the Holy Spirit:

4. ***Feast of Pentecost*** (Lev 23:15): "When the Day of Pentecost had fully come, they were all with one accord in one place. And suddenly there came a sound from heaven, as of a rushing mighty wind, and it filled the whole house where they were sitting. Then there appeared to them divided tongues, as of fire, and one sat upon each of them. And they were all filled with the Holy Spirit and began to speak with other tongues, as the Spirit gave them utterance." (Acts 2:1-4) The Holy Spirit has enabled people to write the New Testament Scriptures, spread the gospel for two thousand years, and lead multitudes to salvation. This is the summer and perfect time to get saved, serve the Lord, bring Him much fruit and get ready for the rapture, which is coming next!

The ***fall feasts*** are yet to come. These feasts are about to happen in a very near future:

5. ***Feast of Trumpets*** (Lev 23:24): **Rapture!** "Behold, I tell you a mystery: we shall not all sleep, but we shall all be changed – in the moment, in the twinkling of an eye, at the last trumpet. For the trumpet will sound, and the dead will be raised incorruptible, and we shall be changed." (1 Cor. 15:51, 52) The rapture is believed to happen during the last of these trumpets. One shouldn't wait for only the Lord knows this time. For the Lord has said that at a time we are not expecting He is going to come. From now on, rapture can happen any time and it is up to us to be ready!

6. ***Feast of Atonement*** (Lev 23:27): **Messiah's Second Coming!** "And in that day His feet will stand on the Mount of Olives, which faces Jerusalem on the east. And the Mount of Olives shall be split in two, from east to west, making a very large valley; half of the mountain shall move toward the north and half of it toward the south." (Zechariah 14:4) Read more on this account from Zachariah 14 & Revelation 19:11-21. It is believed by many that the church is going to come with Jesus at this time.

7. ***Feast of Tabernacles*** (Lev 23:34): **Messiah's Millennial Reign or the Day of the Lord!** "The seventh angel blew his trumpet, and there were loud voices in heaven saying: "The kingdom of the world has become the kingdom of our Lord and of His Messiah, and He will reign forever and ever!" (Revelation 11:15 HCSB) Jesus with His church are going to reign for one thousand years. Later, the church is going to continue to be forever with the Lord!

II

Upon studying Revelation, Daniel, and Joel, I have been faced with the reality of some stunning facts and the days we are in. We are in the "last days" as some may express. We are in the last days right before the Day of the Lord. We are in between 'the sixth angel with the sixth trumpet' and 'the seventh angel with the seventh trumpet.' To be exact, we are about to witness the 'grand finale' events, which are written in the book of Revelation. Just as it is written: "As the days of Noah were, so the coming of the Son of Man will be. For in those days before the flood they were eating and drinking, marrying and giving in marriage, until the day Noah boarded the ark. They didn't know until the flood came and swept them all away. So this is the way the coming of the Son of Man will be: Then two men will be in the field: one will be taken and one left. Two women will be grinding at the mill: one will be taken one left. Therefore be alert, since you don't know what day your Lord is coming. But know this: if the homeowner had known what time the thief was coming, he would have stayed alert and not let his house be broken into. This is why you also must be ready, because the Son of Man is coming at an hour you do not expect."(Matthew 24:37-44 HCSB)

This is so true of our time. The Son of Man is coming at an hour we do not expect! Revelation is happening right before our eyes! The saddest fact is that the majority of Christian people are in deep slumber and busy with their lives. Some are aware, but they are not sure of what to do. Others, do not even want to hear about it. Only a few are prepared or getting prepared to meet the Bridegroom. At time of Noah, only eight souls were saved. Is it possible that only a few may enter the promised arch?

At the beginning of Revelation 8:1, the seventh seal has been broken by the Lamb. Six angels have blown their six trumpets since then. At the time of writing this chapter (April, 2015), sixth angel's trumpet events are taking place as of Revelation 9:13-21. The seventh angel with the seventh seal is to be blown next: "The seventh angel blew his trumpet, and there were loud voices in heaven saying: "The kingdom of the world has become the kingdom of our Lord and of His Messiah, and He will reign forever and ever!" (Revelation 11:15 HCSB) The seventh trumpet is not a trumpet for the rapture. It is the final trumpet, at which Jesus is going to put an end to man's six years of rule and start His seventh year of rule. It is called the Messiah's Millennial Reign or the Feast of Tabernacles (Lev 23:34). Here we see God's mystery in first chapter of Genesis and His instruction to observe the Sabbath, the seventh day of the week.

In order to better understand this chapter, I recommend you read Joel chapter 2, whole book of Revelation and Daniel chapter 12. Also, please refer to the Bible constantly to make a connection to what is happening. Let's take a closer look at these seven angels with their seven trumpets in Revelation 8-11. I am using the text from HCSB:

- *Revelation 8:7:* It is World War I: Both Russians and Germans have had a "Scorched Earth" policy. This created burning of earth, trees and grass. "The first angel blew his trumpet, and hail and fire, mixed with blood, were hurled to the earth. So a third of the earth was burned up, a third of the trees were burned up, and all the green grass was burned up."

- *Revelation 8:8-9:* It is World War II: 'Burning Mountain' is the first atomic bomb used on Japan in Hiroshima and Nagasaki, they were by the sea. It is believed that during World War II, a third of the ships were destroyed and most of the people on the ships died. "The second angel blew his trumpet, and something like a great mountain ablaze with fire was hurled into the sea. So a third of the sea became blood, a third of the living creatures in the sea died, and third of the ships were destroyed."

- *Revelation 8:10-11:* It is the Chernobyl atomic electrical station explosion in 1984: 'Chernobyl' is a combination of two words from old Slavic dialect which interprets as 'bitter plant or wormwood'. Many people especially children have been effected. The rivers and lakes have become radioactive. People have been using the water for the watering, drinking and livestock raising. The devastation of the explosion is not obvious to the naked eye, for the poisoning has come in hidden water and air pollution of which people have developed sicknesses and later death. "The third angel blew his trumpet, and a great star, blazing like torch, fell from heaven. It fell on a third of the rivers and springs of water. The name of the star is Wormwood, and a third of the waters became wormwood. So, many of the people died from waters, because they had been made bitter."

- *Revelation 8:12:* It is the eruption of Mt. Pinatubo in Philippines in 1991: During its eruption a third of the moon and sun was covered due to the eruption cloud. It changed the weather around the globe, too. "The fourth angel blew his trumpet, and a third of the sun was struck, a third of the moon, and a third of the stars, so that a third of them were darkened. A third of the day was without light, and the night as well."

- *Revelation 9:1-12:* It is Operation Desert Storm in 1991: Italy has called this operation 'an operation of locusts.' American helicopters are a close description of the locusts and their ability to shoot and use precision weapons; therefore, no damage was done to the earth. Torment of scorpion is the fear of death. A great smoke has been created by setting on fire around six hundred (610) oil wells. Saddam Hussein was the ruler of Iraq at that time. Saddam means a destroyer. "The fifth angel blew his trumpet, and I saw a star that had fallen from heaven to earth. The key to the shaft of the abyss was given to him. He opened the shaft of the abyss, and smoke came up out of the shaft like smoke from a great furnace so that the sun and the air were darkened by the smoke from the shaft. Then out of the smoke locusts came to the earth, and power was given to them like the power that scorpions have on the earth. They told not to harm the grass of the earth, or any green plant, or any tree, but only people who do not have God's seal on their foreheads. They were not permitted to kill them, but were to torment them for five months; their torment is like the torment caused by a scorpion when it strikes a man. In those days people will seek death and will not find it; they will long to die, but death will flee from them. The appearance of locusts was like horses equipped for battles. On their heads were something like gold crowns; their faces were like men's faces; they had hair like women's hair; their teeth were like lions' teeth; they had chests like iron breastplates; the sound of their wings was like the sound of chariots with many horses rushing into battle; and they had tails with stingers, like scorpions, so that with their tails they had the power to harm people for five months. They had as their king the angel of the abyss; his name in Hebrew is Abaddon, and in Greek he has the name Apollyon. The first woe has passed. There are still two more woes to come after this."

- *Revelation 9:13-21:* It is happening now and began approximately in the beginning of 2014 or even earlier. It involves Iraq, Syria, and Iran or the region of the Euphrates River. ISIS is primary cause of it. The rest is happening before our eyes. "Hour, day, month, and year" mean that four significant things are to happen in that region. How soon the predetermined events are to be completed is not known, nor their outcome to the region nor the rest of the world. The rest of description is exactly the description of machinery and equipment used by ISIS. About a third of the people involved are to die. Two hundred million is the estimated population of that region practicing Islam. Thus, it gives us the source of the troops, they are going to be Islamic in nature, just as we witness through ISIS. "The sixth angel blew his trumpet. From the four horns of the gold alter that is before God, I heard a voice say to the sixth angel who had the trumpet, "Release the four angels bound at the great river Euphrates." So the four angels who were prepared for the hour, day, month, and year were released to kill a third of the human race. The number of mounted troops was 200 million; I heard their number. This is how I saw the horses in my vision: The horsemen had breastplates that were fiery red, hyacinth blue, and sulfur yellow. The heads of the horses were like lions' heads, and from their mouth came fire, smoke and sulfur. A third of the human race was killed by these three plaques – by the fire, the smoke, and the sulfur that came from their mouths. For the power of the horses is in their mouths and in their tails, because their tails, like snakes, have heads, and they inflict injury with them. The rest of the people, who were not killed by these plagues, did not repent of the works of their hands to stop worshiping demons and idols of gold, silver, bronze, stone, and wood, which are not able to see, hear, or walk. And they did not repent of their murders, their sorceries, their sexual immorality, or their thefts."

- *Revelation 11:15-19:* This is the final trumpet that is going to seal the end of man's rule and start the beginning of the Lord's Millennium Rule or the day of the Lord. "The seventh angel blew his trumpet, and there were loud voices in heaven saying: "The kingdom of the world has become the kingdom of our Lord and of His Messiah, and He will reign forever and ever!" The 24 elders, who were seated before God on their thrones, fell on their faces and worshiped God saying: We thank You, Lord God, the Almighty, who is and who was, because You have taken Your great power and have begun to reign. The nations were angry, but Your wrath has come. The time has come for the dead to be judged, and to give the reward to Your servants the prophets, to the saints, and to those who fear Your name, both small and great, and the time has come to destroy those who destroy the earth. God's sanctuary in heaven was opened, and the ark of His Covenant appeared in His sanctuary. There were lightning, rumblings, thunders, an earthquake, and severe hail."

Upon observing and studying Revelation, I have noticed that it has a relatively chronological order. It sometimes stops to give more clarification of certain events. If the seventh angel with the seventh trumpet in chapter 11 is the last trumpet which ends men's rule on earth and starts the Lord's millennium; then between the sixth and the seventh trumpets, there is a period of time for the following events: completion of sixth trumpet's events, the mighty angel with the small scroll (Rev. 10), the two witnesses (Rev. 11:1-14), the woman with the child and dragon (Rev. 12), the beast and his mark (Rev 13), bowls of judgment and battle of Armageddon (Rev. 16), judgment of Babylon the prostitute and the scarlet beast (Rev.17-18), and the rapture (wedding of the Lord and His Church.) It is believed that all of this is going to be accomplished in a period of seven years!

III

"Blow the trumpet in Zion, and sound an alarm in My holy mountain! Let all the inhabitants of the land tremble; for the day of the LORD is coming, for it is at hand: A day of darkness and gloominess, a day of clouds and thick darkness, like the morning clouds spread over the mountains." (Joel 2:1, 2a) Here we see that the trumpet of alarm needs to be sounded on God's mountain (or churches) to warn all people about the approaching of the Day of the Lord. Are we ready to face this day with boldness? It is something not to be taken lightly. It is the day of fear and trembling. While studying the book of Joel, I have noticed that the text of Joel 2:1-10 seems like compressed Revelation chapters 8 & 9. God has given us enough warning through birth pains of His second coming in those two Scriptures.

Further in the book of Joel, we see more clues and signs of the Day of the Lord approach: "And I will show wonders in the heavens and in the earth: blood and fire and pillars of smoke. The sun shall be turned into darkness, and the moon into blood, before the coming of the great and awesome day of the LORD." (Joel 2:30, 31) We have witnessed verse 30 in many ways already. It is a little mix of Revelation 8 & 9 and Joel 2:2-10. Verse 31 is about to be completely finished. We see it in the tetrad or the set of four blood moons that happen on the four Jewish holidays. The first one came in spring of 2014 on Jewish Passover and the last is to happen in fall of 2015 in September on the Jewish feast of Tabernacles. I believe the last blood moon out of these four blood moons, is the last warning by God of His approaching day. We should really be awakened and check our readiness. Putting books of Joel and Revelation together, we are dangerously out of time. These moons are God's way to let us know that things are at the end and that we have not much time left. These moons signify us to stop worrying about earthly matters and start paying closer attention to inner readiness and the Bible. Now is the time to wake up and smell the reality of the approaching climax of the days prior to the Day of the Lord, the rapture and final chapters of the book of Revelation.

The very next last sign is given to us in Revelation 12, "A great sign appeared in heaven: a woman clothed with the sun, with the moon under her feet, a crown of 12 stars on her head. She was pregnant and cried out in labor and agony to give birth." (Rev 12:1, 2 HCSB) This sign is getting very close, for it takes place in September 2017. It is a sign in heaven. There is a constellation of a virgin; twelve stars are going to make her crown in the form of a lion; the moon is going to be under her feet; the sun is going to stay in her background and cloth the virgin; and Jupiter is going to circulate around her abdominal area within a nine month period. She is to give birth to the male child who is to rule the nations. Jupiter is the largest planet and considered the king of the planets. It is "a great sign in heaven" indeed! It is another of God's ways to tell us where we are time wise! Chapter 12 is in mid Revelations. We are here and in the middle of great finale which is approaching fast and we are not aware. When things are going to start happening one after another for many it will be too late. Just as Jesus has illustrated in the parable of ten virgins to tell us to be ready for this event. It is time to heed the message from the Lord that 'we are at hand' or 'right before the door' and the rapture is closer than we think.

In Revelation (10:6c & 7 HCSB), we read that "There will no longer be an interval of time (sometime after the sixth trumpet in Rev 9:13-21), but in the days of the sound of the seventh angel, when he will blow his trumpet, then God's hidden plan (kingdom of Lord and Messiah Rev 11:15-19) will be completed, as He announced to His servants the prophets." (words in parenthesis are mine) In other words, sometime after the sixth trumpet has been blown, there is going to be a starting point when there will no longer be spacing between the events which are written after Revelation 9. If before, the birth contractions have been reasonably spaced out, they are no longer going to have the rest period, but all events are going to follow one after another as planned by God. At the time of my writing this book, I believe that we live shortly after the sixth angel, which has already blown his trumpet. The next trumpet will be blown by the seventh angel. It is going to be the last trumpet at which the Day of the Lord is going to happen.

IV

We see another sure sign of our time, the quality of our spiritual condition and devastative defect of God's people: "...And one said to the man clothed in linen, who was above the waters of the river, "How long shall the fulfillment of these wonders be? ... that it shall be for a time, times, and half a time; and when the power of the holy people has been completely shattered, all these things shall be finished." (Daniel 12: 6 & 7b) Apostle Paul describes this devastation in the following way: "But know this, that in the last days perilous times will come: for men will be lovers of themselves, lovers of money, boasters, proud, blasphemers, disobedient to parents, unthankful, unholy, unloving, unforgiving, slanderers, without self-control, brutal, despisers of good, traitors, headstrong, haughty, lovers of pleasure rather than lovers of God, having a form of godliness but denying its power. And from such people turn away! For of this sort are those who creep into households and make captives of gullible women loaded down with sins, led away by various lusts, always learning and never able to come to the knowledge of the truth. Let no one deceive you by any means, for that Day will not come <u>unless the falling away comes first</u>..." (2 Timothy 3:1-7 & 2 Thessalonians 2:3a)

Thus we see through several scriptures that people, who are considered to be God's, are going to be in a state of contradiction to God's expected quality, prior to the second coming of Christ. Jesus' words reinforce this point even further: "Nevertheless, when the Son of Man comes, will He really find faith on the earth?" (Luke 18:8b)

Jesus gives us even more details: "Take heed that no one deceives you. For many will come in My name, saying, 'I am the Christ,' and will deceive many. And you will hear of wars and rumors of wars. See that you are not troubled; for all these things must come to pass, but the end is not yet. For nation will rise against nation, and kingdom against kingdom. And there will be famines, pestilences, and earthquakes in various places. All these are the beginning of sorrows. Then they will deliver you up to tribulation and kill you, and you will be hated by all nations for My name's sake. And then <u>many will be offended, will betray one another, and will hate one another. Then many false prophets will rise up and deceive many. And because lawlessness will abound, the love of many will grow cold. But he who endures to the end shall be saved</u>. And this gospel of the kingdom will be preached in all the world as a witness to all the nations, and then the end will come." (Matthew 24:4b -14)

The power of the holy people are their holiness, righteousness, faithfulness to Christ, obedience and abidance to His Word, and separation from the works of this world. Even though, Scripture is telling us about the falling away or a change in the quality of His people and presence of deception, His bride must be different. It must be holy. I am not sure that we are as holy and pure as we ought to be. Matter of fact, we are not ready. If the rapture is to happen at this moment, a staggering amount of Christians would be left behind. It saddens me to see and know, that most of the believers think that they are qualified and ready for the rapture. But their belief is not grounded on the Scripture, but on puffed up promises that have been taught on lies and twisting of the Scripture. The Bible has warned us about deceptions, false teachers and prophets, great falling away and being left behind. Are we for sure travelling on the safe boat and in the right direction? One degree to the right or left and we can miss our desired destination. There is no room for any mistakes, for any mistake is eternal.

V

"Blow the trumpet in Zion, and sound an alarm in My holy mountain! Let all the inhabitants of the land tremble; for the day of the Lord is coming, for it is at hand. For the Day of the Lord is great and very terrible; who can endure it? Now, therefore," says the Lord, "turn to Me with all your heart, with fasting, with weeping, and with mourning." So rend your heart, and not your garments; return to the Lord your God, for He is gracious and merciful, slow to anger, and of great kindness; and He relents from doing harm. Who knows if He will turn and relent, and leave a blessing behind Him – a grain offering and a drink offering for the Lord your God? Blow the trumpet in Zion, consecrate a fast, call a sacred assembly; gather the people, sanctify the congregation, assemble the elders, gather the children and nursing babes; <u>let the bridegroom go out from his chamber, and the bride from her dressing room</u>." (Joel 2:1, 11b, 12-16)

Let's look closer at these verses:

❖ **Blow the trumpet in Zion:**

   a. Two times in one chapter and in the directions for taking action, we see the order to 'blow the trumpet in Zion.'

119

Repetition shows importance and signals us to pay attention – there is something we need to heed and do. While interpreting pharaoh's dreams, Joseph says the following: "Because the dream was given twice to Pharaoh, it means that the matter has been determined by God, and He will soon carry it out." (Genesis 41:32 HCSB)

b. Zion is God's holy mountain. Jerusalem is built on it. Jerusalem is a holy place chosen by God. "Beautiful in elevation, the joy of the whole earth, is Mount Zion on the sides of the north, the city of the great King." (Psalm 48:2) Where else does God dwell? He dwells in his church.

c. Therefore, we have a command to tell His church of the importance of the day we live in. We need to sound the alarm of His coming, everyone must know that His day is approaching and we need to be ready and prepared. For the wedding is at hand: *"let the bridegroom go out from his chamber, and the bride from her dressing room."*

❖ **Turn to Me with all your heart, with fasting, with weeping, and with mourning:**

a. Here we see God's command to turn to Him with all the heart.
b. Turn to Him with fasting
c. Turn to Him with weeping and with mourning.

It looks like God wants us to be ready for His coming by preparing through fasting, prayer and repenting. As we have discussed above, we are not ready to meet Him the way we are now. We have a spiritual defect, our power is completely shattered. We cannot see God without holiness. The power of holy people is their holiness, "Pursue peace with everyone, and <u>holiness – without it no one will see the Lord</u>. See to it that no one falls short of the grace of God and that no root of bitterness springs up, causing trouble and by it, defiling many." (Hebrew 12:14, 15 HCSB)

The Lord has known the devastation of His people in the last days at the time of Daniel and Joel. Also, He knows that we are in big trouble and that we cannot do it alone. This is why He wants us to blow the trumpet or tell others, fast and cry out to Him. Only He has the power to produce the fruit in us necessary to meet Him and finish His harvest: "I am the vine, you are the branches. He who abides in Me, and I in him, bears much fruit; <u>for without Me you can do nothing</u>. If anyone does not abide in Me, he is cast out as a branch and is withered; and they gather them and throw them into the fire, and they are burned. If you abide in Me, and My words abide in you, you will ask what you desire, and it shall be done for you. By this My Father is glorified, that you bear much fruit; so you will be My disciples." (John 15:5-8)

Our Lord is very merciful. He doesn't only warn us, but has a plan to get us ready. When we read further in the chapter of Joel, we find the following verse: "The LORD raises His voice in the presence of His army. His camp is very large; those who carry out His command are powerful. Indeed, the Day of the LORD is terrible and dreadful, who can endure it?" (Joel 2:11 HCSB) He has prepared us an army through which He plans to use in the last days. He needs this army, for He does many things through His church and His people on earth.

VI

<u>Word on Rapture</u>: It is wise from now on to be ready for the rapture. I couldn't find any proof of the pre-tribulation rapture, nor do I suggest that we shouldn't be prepared for the early rapture. It is wise to be prepared for both scenarios. I can't deny a great possibility that the church is going to be here during the beast's time. There is no information on the amount of time the Lord's bride is going to endure the beast's days. Revelation gives us just some hints of the possibility of the church being present during most of the Revelation events: "And he was permitted to wage war against the saints and conquer them. If anyone has ear, he should listen: If anyone is destined for captivity, into captivity he goes. If anyone is to be killed with a sword, with a sword he will be killed. Here is the endurance and the faith of the saints." (Rev. 13:7a, 9, 10 HSCB)

Also, in chapter 12, we see another evidence of the possible church's presence and persecution: "So the dragon was furious with the woman and left to wage war against the rest of her offspring – those who keep the commandments of God and have the testimony about Jesus." (Rev. 12:17 HCSB) Paul writes, "Let no one deceive you by any mean; for that Day will not come unless the falling away comes first, and the man of sin is revealed, the son of perdition, who opposes and exalts himself above all that is called God or what is worshiped, so that he sits as God in the temple of God, showing himself that he is God." (2 Thessalonians 2:3, 4)

There is a great indication that the church is not going to be present during the bowls of judgment and possibly during the judgment of the Babylon (Rev. 16-18). "Then I heard another voice from heaven: Come out of her, My people, so that you will not share in her sins, or receive any of her plaques. For her sins are piled up to heaven, and God has remembered her crimes." (Rev. 18:4, 5 HCSB)

Are we prepared for an early rapture? Are we prepared to endure what is coming, if the rapture time is going to be postponed? Are our family, children, husband, relatives prepared? We do not know which hour Jesus comes for His bride, but we must be prepared to meet Him and possibly face the things we hope to avoid.

➤ **CONCLUSION:** The day of the Lord is right around the corner! It is dangerously and excitedly here! Are we ready? There are many things that need to be done in a very short period of time. Let's continue on reading to see what can be done. And let's start on the command! Let others know that Christ is coming and it is time to get ready. Also, tell other ladies about this book, so they can read and learn what they can do to maximize their preparation and readiness. But, please don't stop at this. Knowledge is of no use, if one doesn't act upon it.

➤ **WHAT TO DO:** Read through the book of Revelation, it is easier to understand than many think.

CHAPTER 6

Lord's Very Large
Powerful Army

I

*"The LORD raises His voice in the presence of <u>His army</u>.
His camp is <u>very large</u>; those who carry out His command
are <u>powerful</u>. Indeed, the Day of the LORD is terrible
and dreadful – who can endure it?"* (Joel 2:11 HCSB)

ave you ever thought about this particular verse? Who is Lord's very large powerful army? Why does He raise His voice? Who are those powerful ones that carry out His command? No, this passage is not talking about those people who do the described destruction of the earlier verses (Joel 2:1-10). He is talking about His holy army and gives instructions to do something during such a time as this. I have found an explanation about this army in this passage:

*"The Lord gives the command; the women who proclaim
the good tidings are a great host: kings of armies flee, they
flee, and she who remains at home will divide the spoil!
When you lie down among the sheepfolds, you are like
the wings of a dove covered with silver, and its pinions
with glistening gold. When the Almighty scattered the kings
there, it was snowing in Zalmon."* (Psalm 68:11-14 NASB)

In some of David's psalms we find at least one prophetic verse about Christ. Psalm 68 is believed by many to refer to the glorious second coming of Christ. It is one of the psalms that is hard to translate due to the Hebrew poetry, especially verses 11-14. Interpreters seem to agree that in Hebrew they refer to plural female gender. Regardless, it is written in many Bible versions by omitting the reference to female gender. It is difficult for some to swallow the controversy of the Word of God in this passage.

Is there controversy in these verses? I don't think so. There are many passages in the Bible that seem to be controversial at first or difficult to understand. All Scriptures in the Holy Bible are divine and God breathed. Therefore there can be no mistake in the holy writing. God is sovereign and He is watchful of His Word. Just because something doesn't seem to make sense to a man's understanding, doesn't prove any mistake on God's behalf. It just shows that we lack the proper understanding at a given time. Besides, God's prophetic words are difficult to understand for many. As proof, we have many attempts at interpretation of hidden messages in the books of Revelation, Joel, Daniel and other prophets. Being so, doesn't prove any error, only the fact that we are limited to certain truths until it is divinely opened to us by the Holy Spirit at the timing it is designed to be revealed. Therefore, we have a prophetic passage for women in David's psalm! It is very similar to the above passage from the book of Joel. It is actually a prophetic command that shouldn't be overlooked. If the Lord commands, we must obey. Let's look at it closer:

❖ ***The Lord gives the command:*** There is an order by God for women to do something.

❖ ***The women who proclaim the good tidings are a great host:*** The women are doing what is expected of them by the Lord by caring out His command.

❖ ***Kings of armies flee, they flee:*** When women started to carry out God's command, the kings of armies ran away. If kings of the armies run away, so do their armies! There is no army without the commanders. Who are those armies and their kings? "For our battle is not against flesh and blood, but against the rulers, against the authorities, against the world powers of this darkness, against the spiritual forces of evil in the heavens." (Ephesians 6:12 HCSB)

❖ ***She who remains at home will divide the spoil:*** The woman stays home, but she enjoys the fruits of her victory, she is going to be rewarded for carrying out the Lord's command. Her strength is in the walls of her own home, in her home she is going to see the spoil or the fruit of her obedience to the Lord.

❖ ***When you lie down among the sheepfolds, you are like the wings of a dove covered with silver, and its pinions with glistening gold:*** "The Almighty will be your gold and your finest silver." (Job 22:25 HCSB) There is nothing more precious than God Himself: "Again, the kingdom of heaven is like a merchant seeking beautiful pearls, who, when he had found one pearl of great price, went and sold all that he had and bought it." (Matthew 13:45, 46)

❖ ***When the Almighty scattered the kings there, it was snowing in Zalmon:*** "Then you will delight in the Almighty and lift up your face to God. You will pray to Him, and He will hear you, and you will fulfill your vows. When you will make a decision, it will be carried out, and light will shine on your ways. When others are humiliated and you say, "Lift them up," God will save the humble. He will even rescue the guilty one, who will be rescued by the purity of your hands." (Job 22:26-30 HCSB) God is going to use our fruit of obedience to save many, and we will delight in our work. For out of our work God is going to build heavenly city. Do not underestimate obedience to His call, "Now his daughter was Sheerah, <u>who built</u> Lower and Upper Beth Horon and Uzzen Sheerah. (1 Chronicles 7:24)

II

The Lord has given His command to the women at three different times, which has created three movements:

1. **At Jesus' resurrection**: "But the angel answered and said to the women, "Do not be afraid, for I know that you seek Jesus who was crucified. He is not here; for He is risen, as He said. Come, see the place where the Lord lay. And go quickly and tell His disciples that He is risen from the dead, and indeed He is going before you into Galilee; there you will see Him. Behold, I have told you. So they went out quickly from the tomb with fear and great joy, and ran to bring His disciples word." (Matthew 28:5-8) Since that day, we see in Acts and Paul's epistles that God has been calling women to salvation and usefulness in spreading the Good News.

2. **In the beginning of 1800 until present**: Multitudes of women have spread the Good News through involvement in missions in different creative ways, including preaching and teaching. Most of them are forgotten and not spoken of, but they are on God's honor list. God has used them where He could not use men. In many countries, customs didn't allow men to speak to women. So, women missionaries have been a tremendous contribution to save female souls and children, which otherwise wouldn't be reached. Also, where people couldn't trust and listen to a man, they have listened to a woman without any dread. In addition, many cultures have been closed to any new religious ideas, and other means needed to be used to get the doors opened. Women have been far outnumbered in mission fields doing things that seemed insignificant to men, or that men never had patience or right opportunities to do the tasks. Women

have been used by God as doors or ice breakers where men couldn't succeed at all. Women have interpreted Scripture into different languages; used in the medical area to help the sick; work with orphans, etc. They've been used in teaching women, children and even men: Bible and other necessary survival and important fields like hygiene, basic medical needs, agriculture, sewing, etc. In addition, they have been used in variety of humanitarian and service work, thus opening doors for spreading Jesus' teaching.

Matter of fact, women have outnumbered men in obedience to the great commission to spread the gospel. Most of the gospel has been spread due to their faithfulness, commitment and versatility. They have endured a lot and suffered much. But the most difficult has been to stand the opposition of many Christian men, who thought that women should belong only to their own homes. At the present, women still outnumber men in mission field and church work. Men see work in preaching, women see it in doing and living it. They are the feet and hands of Jesus. They touch hurt and hungry souls on individual basis and get personal and close to the people. Through their work, many souls have come to Christ, for preaching alone can't do what Jesus wants us to do. Many people can't see the gospel without practical application of the good Samaritan principle. Women are ministering mostly to women and children. Men cannot minister in the same way that women do. Denying women the right to spread the gospel, is the same thing as removing hands and feet from the body of Christ. Women get outside of church walls and reach out to people who otherwise would not be able to come to church for the gospel.

3. **Last call:** The last call is now. It is to finish the harvest: "The Lord raises His voice in the presence of His army and gives a command; the women who carry out His command are powerful, they are a great host and make a very large camp.

128

Because of their obedience, they will delight in the Almighty and lift their faces to God. They will pray to Him and He will hear them and He will rescue many by the purity of their hands." (combination of Joel 2:11, Psalm 68:11-14 & Job 22:26-30) There are things He wants us to do, the things He can't do without women. Women can and should stand up for the souls of many through prayer and fasting, without which the harvest is going to be skimpy. The Lord wants to harvest a bountiful harvest and He depends on us greatly because He has given us an ability to fight the enmity of our enemy. In the last chapter, we have learned that many are not ready, for in the last days 'the power of the holy people has been completely shattered.' We have very little time left. Much is needed to be done: praying, fasting, and reaching out where God calls us to. I believe, God is going to use women mightily in the last days, if they humble and seek His face.

III

Judith and Esther are two captivating books of the Bible with accounts of two godly Jewish brave women taking risk by standing up to the task of saving their people. Their men haven't been equipped for the job, for those jobs only women could accomplish. As we read the book of Esther, we see an interesting and intense story is taking place: the plan of Haman to destroy the entire nation of Jews. That's quite a daring undertaking, indeed. It reminds me of satan, who has the same plans as Haman's. He knows that his days are numbered and that he has lost, and that what is written about his end is true. This knowledge makes him furious, for there are people who are going to have a different outcome from his. There are people who are going to go to heaven and spend their eternity in peace and joy, with no suffering and no regrets. The enemy is having a plan to destroy them on their way and have some of them share his fate. "Be sober, be vigilant; because your adversary the devil walks about like a roaring lion, seeking whom he may devour." (1st Peter 5:8) Satan is worse than Haman. His cunning act of deception in the Garden of Eden has taken from us: the true rulership and authority over everything, peace, joy, love, and eternity. Thanks to Jesus, we have been able to regain some of it back. Most importantly, through Jesus' sacrifice, we can have salvation from eternal condemnation.

Esther has been placed by God between her people and the king, her husband. She has been the only hope and solution for the Jews' trouble, at that time. No man could save them. Actually, because of one man's loyalty to God, Mordechai, Haman decided to execute his dirty plan. Esther seems like the only one who can change the verdict by petitioning before the king. There was only one problem, the king hasn't called Esther to his presence for thirty days. It is suicidal to face the king without his consent and desire. So, "Esther sent this reply to Mordecai: "Go and assemble all the Jews who can be found in Susa and fast for me. Don't eat or drink for three days, night and day. I and my female servants will also fast in the same way. After that, I will go to the king even if it is against the law. If I perish, I perish."" (Esther 4:15, 16 HCSB) What was the outcome? "And the king said to her, "What do you wish, Queen Esther? What is your request? It shall be given to you – up to half the kingdom!" (Esther 5:3) After three days of fasting, the king's heart turned to Esther with favor and approval! Her bravery and right approach had saved an entire nation of Jews and prevented the bloodshed of a multitude of innocent people including children!

We sometimes forget that God has provided us with simple tools. We need to use them in order to reap their benefits. We use them, God acts on our behalf. We are very weak, but He is strong. We need to unleash His greatness through the tools He has given us. We need to know what is available to us and how to claim what is ours. Speaking things into our lives, believing and hoping are not going to intimidate satan, nor are they going to move God to the point of making a huge noise and change. God wants sacrifice on an alter, for if there is no sacrifice – there is no need for fire. "Then the fire of the LORD fell and consumed the burnt sacrifice, and the wood and the stones and the dust, and it licked up the water that was in trench." (1 Kings 18:38) We need to come to the thrown of God in the manner He teaches us and then receive out of His hands the desirable requests. Outside of God's hands, we can't get anything. We are poor, but He is rich.

Let's look at what moves God and what kind of sacrifice He is looking to get from us, for He loves to answer our prayers. He actually waits for us to act first. There are tools He has given to us that make Him move on our behalf. He sees them as sacrifices on the alter which He is waiting to send His fire to devour. They are prayer, fasting, and complete obedience to the Word of God. Those are the things that have made the difference for all saints. Blessings come to us through obedience to His Word. Battles and strongholds are won through prayer and fasting. Let's look at them closer through the book and story of Esther:

❖ **Fasting:** Why fast? Fasting enables us to reach the needed results in a shorter time than just a prayer by itself. When one has no time to spare or when the petition is urgent and of great importance, fasting is the way to go. Fasting has been a practice of old. It has been practiced by prophets, Pharisees and the rest of Jews. It has been used by the disciples frequently and with great success. Jesus has fasted forty days before beginning His three year ministry. Unfortunately, in the time of plenty, we forget to practice it. We have forgotten how powerful it can be against the schemes of the enemy. It is the most effective weapon in the battles in the spiritual realms. Satan is afraid of our prayers, but he trembles when we add a fast to them.

There are books out there on fasting. In many of them, you can find wonderful encouragement and practical information on how-to's, physical and spiritual benefits and different kinds of fasts. Check your local library for books on fasting, before committing to buy one. Approach reasonably, especially if you have health issues and have never fasted before. Word of caution: if you want to fast more than three days on only water, see books which describe the process. One must need to know what to expect, how to prepare before the fast, and how to get off the fast. If you have some serious medical issues, talking to your doctor is advisable. Long fasts are not for everyone, but several half a day or one day fasts are doable.

If fasting is difficult and/or impossible due to hard work and/or health, partial fasts can be used. These are fasts that exclude certain foods. Daniel fasted by excluding some foods and eating the others. Things to consider excluding: coffee, white flour products, store bought juices, meat and dairy. People fast on freshly squeezed juices and/or raw vegetables and fruits. Others, skip just a meal or substitute with a liquid.

Personally, I struggle with fasting. But with the Lord's help, I managed to do several half day fasts, ¾ day fasts, whole day fasts, one three day fast and one seven day fast. All were with no food and just some water. It is more of a battle within the head, then hunger. I always ask God to help me fast. It has taken me several attempts before I could accomplish my three day and seven day fasts. I have read books on fasting prior to accomplishing seven day fast. As I am writing this chapter, I am in prayer before the Lord to give me strength for another three day fast, which I need to do.

When you start a fast, come to the Lord in at least a short prayer. Tell Him of your petition and ask Him to help you to fast. At the end of the fast, thank Him for helping you fast and again bring your request to the Lord in prayer. It is recommended to be more in prayer and the Word reading throughout the day during the fast. But, if you can't run away from the business of your life, fast anyway. Better to fast the way you can, than not at all. Any effort on our part is better than none at all.

❖ **Two banquets to the King:** After three days of fasting, Esther has won King Ahasuerus' approval and he has met her with the following words, "What do you wish, Queen Esther? What is your request? It shall be given to you – up to half the kingdom!" The queen didn't blurt out her request in a haste. The urgency and importance of her request was extremely sensitive. If not handled in the proper and wise way, it may cost her and her nation dearly. So, she requested the king come to her two banquets. Her husband is too great of a man of importance. One queen has been disqualified. She needs to act carefully and please the king, or she might share the fate of Vashti, as well. Only after knowing for sure that the king's heart is with her and that he is ready to receive her petition does she bring her request to him.

Our Heavenly King is far greater in majesty then the king of ancient Persia and Media. The wrong teaching about grace has removed from us the reverence and respect He deserves. "Clouds and thick darkness surround Him; righteousness and justice are the foundation of His throne. Fire goes before Him and burns up His foes on every side. His lightning lights up the world; the earth sees and trembles. The mountains melt like wax at the presence of the LORD – at the presence of the LORD of all the earth. The heavens proclaim His righteousness; all the peoples see His glory. All who serve carved images, those who boast in idols, will be put to shame. All the gods must worship Him." (Psalm 97:2-7 HCSB)

What two kinds of banquets can we prepare before Him? *"But on this one will I look: on him who is poor and of a contrite spirit, and who trembles at My word."* (Isaiah 66:2b):

1. ***Poor and contrite spirit:*** We need to look for the example of the King of kings, Jesus. He has shown us the way to the Father and His life is the pure example of how we ought to be. After being baptized by John the Baptist, "suddenly a voice came from heaven, saying, "This is My beloved Son, in whom I am well pleased."" (Matthew 3:17) Why was God pleased with Jesus? Because Jesus, "who, being in the form of God, did not consider it robbery to be equal with God, but <u>made Himself of no reputation</u>, taking the form of a bondservant, and coming in the likeness of men. And being found in appearance as a man, He humbled Himself and became obedient to the point of death, even the death of the cross." (Philippians 2:5-8)

   Jesus told us the following: "Come to Me, all you who labor and heavy laden, and I will give you rest. Take my yoke upon you, and learn from Me, for I am gentle and lowly in heart; and you will find rest for your souls. For My yoke is easy, and My load is light." (Matthew 11:28-30) He has left us this example. We are to learn to be humble and gentle like Him. This is how He is with His Father. He refused to do things His own way, but has given His will to His Father. We receive peace which is given by God only through submission of our will to His. 'Father, let your will be done not ours.' Now, that's a feast! For "God resists the proud, but gives grace to the humble." (1 Peter 5:5c) Humbleness before God is demonstrated through acceptance of His will, obedience to His Word, and acknowledgement of our need for Him.

2. ***Tremble at God's Word:*** "Do not think that I came to destroy the Law or the Prophets. I did not come to destroy but to fulfil."(Matthew 5:17) Again we go to Jesus as an example. Jesus had to obey every tittle. He didn't use His creativity, He had submitted to the Law and the Word of God. We see God's heart for His Word in this passage:

"For you have magnified Your word above all Your name."
(Psalm 138:2b)

It is a turn off to God, when His people continually disrespect His Word. Grace has been given to us to live out His Word and not to break it. If our understanding of grace is a permission and an excuse to sin, we have failed grace. It is not pleasant to God and dangerous for us. "But be doers of the word, and not hearers only, deceiving yourselves. (James 1:22) We will not move far with our prayers, for God can't hear us when we are disobedient to His Word, "One who turns away his ear from hearing the law, even his prayer is an abomination." (Proverbs 28:9)

I cannot believe, that I live in the days when I am being out argued by modern Christians that sin is OK! Let's return to the obedience and trembling at God's Word. Stop just reading and quoting it. It is time we should seriously consider repenting for trampling His Word and start truly living it and abiding in it. Come to the Lord with fasting, humbleness and repentance. Acknowledge that you have failed to be humble and submissive to His Word, and that you need His help to change. Repent for your pride and disobedience to His Word. Ask Him to help you be the obedient doer of His Word and not just a deceived hearer.

❖ **Petition (or prayer):** "Once again, on the second day while drinking wine, the king asked Esther, "Queen Esther, whatever you ask will be given to you. Whatever you seek, even to half the kingdom, will be done." Queen Esther answered, "If I have obtained your approval, my king, and if the king is pleased, spare my life – this is my request; and spare my people – this is my desire. For my people and I have been sold out to destruction, death, and extermination. If we had merely been sold as male and female slaves, I would have kept silent. Indeed, the trouble wouldn't be worth burdening the king." (Esther 7:2-4 HCSB)

Prayer is a tool of communication with God. We need to go to God with our petitions, daily. There is a cup to be filled with daily persistent prayers and fasting as needed. One pronounced prayer is not going to release a soul out of the enemy's hands. It is going to take several persistent days, weeks, months and sometimes even years of praying until the cup is filled and the Lord starts to act on the petition. One prayer a day is good. Three prayers a day are better. Seven prayers are even better, for the cup is being filled faster. One day of fasting is good. But three one day fasts within three weeks are better. You get the point. Fasting is going to speed up the filling of the petition cup. If your son is lost, take time to do anything and everything to get him found.

I have found in my own practice, that when I pray with Scripture, I get the desirable results faster, too. The Word of God is our spiritual sword. Using it in prayer makes sense, indeed. Be cautious about binding and commanding, etc.; for it is easier to get hurt instead of being helped. Learn to come to God in prayer, fasting and with the right heart, first. God is going to give wisdom when it is needed for binding or commanding after practice and experience in the smaller things first.

- ***Prayer with thanksgiving:*** "Be anxious for nothing, but in everything by <u>prayer</u> and supplication, <u>with thanksgiving</u>, let your requests be made known to God; and the peace of God, which surpasses all understanding, will guard your hearts and minds through Christ Jesus. Let's be believers of the word and not only readers." (Philippians 4:6, 7) For "we know that all things work together for good to those who love God, to those who are called according to His purpose." (Romans 8:28) No matter how tough it gets, let's be thankful and grateful for the things we get in our way. Let's put aside what we think it should be or compare our fate to others. For God works with us for our benefit. "Rejoice always, pray without ceasing, in everything give thanks; for this is the will of God in Christ Jesus for you." (1 Thessalonians 5:16-18)

❖ **Apparel:** "Now it happened on the third day that <u>Esther put on her royal robes and stood in the inner court of the king's palace</u>, across from the king's house, while the king sat on his royal throne in the royal house, facing the entrance of the house. (Esther 5:1)

Esther knew very well how to show up before the king. Just any dress is not going to work. She put on her royal robes. Does our heavenly King require us to be in any different attire? Do Christian women have any guidelines on how to dress? God does care how His people get dressed, especially when they come into His presence. "And you shall make holy garments for Aaron your brother, for glory and for beauty." (Exodus 28:2) Our body is the temple of the Holy Spirit, and therefore, it should be dressed in the way it pleases the Lord, too.

"In like manner also, that the women <u>adorn themselves in modest apparel</u>, with propriety and moderation, not with braided hair or gold or pearls or costly clothing, but, <u>which is proper for women professing godliness</u>, with good works." (1 Timothy 2:9, 10) This verse doesn't suggest for us to neglect normal care of our body and our appearance. It tells us to dress like godly women. Excess in jewelry, make up and wrong clothing may hamper our usefulness to the Lord, create stumbling blocks for many, especially men and may be abominable in the eyes of God. If we are Christians, we should not look like holywood actresses, drunkies just falling off the bar, nor harlots ready to jump into bed at any first wink of a man's eye. Our fashion tastes have been dulled by the media, therefore we need to seek God in this area. He can reveal our fashion short comings. Remember that body piercing, tattooing, and the man's clothing on the woman's body are an abomination to the Lord. "A woman shall not wear anything that pertains to a man, nor shall a man put on a woman's garment, for all who do so are an abomination to the LORD your God." (Deuteronomy 22:5)

Just as Jesus said of us, we must be the light. Our clothing, words and actions speak louder than we think. Therefore, let's put on the light as our overall attire. May we bring glory to God through everything including our clothing.

➢ **CONCLUSION:** Just as Esther, we need to come to our King of kings and Lord of lords. We need to come in humbleness and with a poor and needy spirit, with prayer and fasting. We need to petition before our Lord, for our souls and souls of our husbands, children, relatives and whoever He is going to show us to petition for. Time is short. Many are deceived and not ready. Many are not even believers, yet. Many have gone astray. The harvest is closing in. All grain needs to be gathered. The Lord doesn't want to leave anyone behind. Perhaps, 'the Lord has put us at such a time as this,' to gather the grain where each one of us are. I can only imagine the bountiful of harvest, if every Christian woman, regardless of age and her marital status, will respond to this call! What a great victory for the Lord! It is our time to face the Lord with fasting, weeping, supplication, and petition for our souls and souls of our family. Perhaps, our most significant request at this time should be: 'Lord, we want to live. We want our family to live. Spare us from the enemy. Show us where we are, and what we should do. Prepare and do whatever is necessary to get us from eternal condemnation which is called hell. Time is short. Be merciful, spare our souls.'

CHAPTER 7

The Wisdom of Little and Wise

I

"God has spoken once, twice I have heard this: that power belongs to God. But My people would not heed My voice, and Israel would have none of Me. So I gave them over to their own stubborn heart, to walk in their own counsels. Oh, that My people would listen to Me, that Israel would walk in My ways! I would soon subdue their enemies, and turn My hand against their adversaries." (Psalm 62:11; 81:11-14)

We can't crush the enemy's head, nor bruise it, nor save ourselves apart from God. God is our only source and power, for He does everything by His Spirit. "'Not by might nor by power, but by My Spirit,' says the LORD of hosts." (Zach. 4:6b) Jesus has called Himself the vine and us the branches. As branches can't bear fruit apart from the vine, so we can't do anything apart from God.

Women are weaker vessels, therefore their tactics should be different from the one who is strong. Israel has been a nation which depended on God, unless they turned to idols. If God was on their side, no enemy could overpower them. If God was against them, no effort on their part has ever been successful. God has left us the following illustrations to learn from: *"There are four things which are little on the earth, but exceedingly wise:*

the ants are a people not strong, yet they prepare their food in the summer; the rock badgers are a feeble folk, yet they make their homes in the crags; the locusts have no king, yet they all advance in ranks; the spider skillfully grasps with its hands, and it is in kings' palaces." (Proverbs 30:24-28) Let's go through this verse one section at a time:

❖ **The ants are a people not strong, yet they prepare their food in the summer:**

"I passed by the field of the sluggard, by the vineyard of the man without sense; and behold! It was all overgrown with thistles; its surface was covered with nettles, and its stone wall broken down. And as I gazed at it, I reflected; I saw and learned the lesson: a little sleep, a little slumber, a little folding of the arms to rest – then will poverty come upon you like a highwayman, and want like an armed man." (Proverbs 24:30-34 NAB) This is a description of a lazy person or a person without sense. Such a person can be compared to a butterfly. The butterfly is beautiful, but careless. It would fly from flower to flower all summer long and once cold comes – it dies. It hasn't prepared itself food or shelter and hasn't been able to feed itself and protect itself from cold.

A person with a sense can be compared to an ant. A honey bee is another insect that can be compared to the wisdom of the ant. Both insects work during the summer to feed themselves, their colonies, raise and feed their brood or babies, store food in advance for many cold months of winter, and keep themselves protected from cold.

Jesus illustrated this comparison in a parable of talents. One lazy servant has failed to use his talent by hiding it under ground. When the time has come to meet the master, he was chastised for his laziness and ended up thrown into an outer darkness (or hell): "And cast the unprofitable servant into the outer darkness. There will be weeping and gnashing of teeth." (Matthew 25:30) God doesn't approve of spiritual laziness. The servant with one talent was required only one thing, the only thing he was capable of – the salvation of his own soul. Before one can be worried about doing something for the Lord or saving anyone, one needs to check the inner self: 'Am I saving myself, is the one and only talent that is given to me in use?' "For what profit is it to a man if he gains the whole world, and loses his own soul?"(Matthew 16:26) Before saving others, we need to be actively working on saving ourselves. We need to look through the eyes of the Scripture and check where we are standing. Is what we are building a building at all? Perhaps what we do is nothing less than hiding our talent in the earth. We need to unearth it, clean it and polish it. May the light shine from us. Our transformation can do more work for the Lord than many seemingly important works that we may undertake.

"Therefore take heed how you hear. For whoever has, to him more will be given; and whoever does not have, even what he seems to have will be taken from him." (Luke 8:18) For if one neglected the work of saving one's own soul, and has hid this only one talent under the earth, it is going to be lost. Before one can become a useful soldier in God's army, one must correct all the things where one is lacking and then come into God's army. In His army ranks, people have uniforms, which one must wear daily. This uniform is the whole armor of God. Wear it and do not take it off. It is going to guarantee that one is faithful in using the most important talent, salvation of its' own soul.

- ### *How to go about saving one's own soul?*

1) Pray daily for God to show where change is needed. Also ask Him to put on you the whole armor of God. The prayer may sound like this: 'Lord, please, put on me the armor of God. Gird my loins in truth, cloth me with righteousness as a breastplate, and my feet shod in readiness for the gospel of peace. Help me in all circumstances, hold faith as a shield to quench all the flaming arrows of the evil one. Put on me the helmet of salvation and give me the sword of the Spirit. Help me understand Your Word and read it daily. Help me to pray at every opportunity and daily have prayer with you. Baptize me with the Holy Spirit, so I can pray in the Spirit (if you are not baptized, yet.)'

2) Pray about other things that you think are needed for your salvation and growth. Use prayers based on Scripture. I always pray the following: 'Lord, help me to finish the race. May I enter through the narrow gate, so I will be saved. Have mercy on me. Save my soul and help me to go through whatever I may face and stay faithful to You. Show me where I need to change. May I not miss Your coming or the rapture. Never take my life, when I am not prepared.'

3) Read and study the Word of God daily. David has said: "I hate the double-minded, but I love Your law." (Psalm 119:113) In Russian translation, it would be something like this: "I hate the man-made knowledge, but I love Your law." It is basically telling us that the Word of God is enough. It is going to work with us personally on a daily basis. Stay away from all those man-made studies. You are to learn how to serve God and be saved, and not how to accumulate knowledge. Knowledge alone is not going to save you. One needs to apply the truth daily.

4) The prayer and Bible study are going to produce many changes. Once God is going to work, He will show you where and how to change.

5) Walk in repentance. "If we say that we have no sin, we deceive ourselves, and the truth is not in us. If we confess our sins, He is faithful and just to forgive us our sins and to cleanse us from all unrighteousness. If we say that we have not sinned, we make Him a liar, and His word is not is us." (1 John 1:8-10) The blood of Jesus cleanses us after we verbally confess our sins and sincerely repent. Since we fall into sin, we are in need of repentance, for nothing unclean and no sin is permissible in heaven. The closer I have gotten to the Lord, His light started to expose all my sins which I was ignorant of before. Therefore, I repent the moment my words or thoughts come short of Him. Also, daily before retiring for the day, I look through my day and confess to Him anywhere I have come short. Also, I ask Him to cleanse me from any sins that I may be blind to and show me anywhere I fall short, so I can change. We need to run from sin, for sin makes great harm here and is going to interfere with our salvation if not dealt with on a timely manner. Sin hurts us and others.

6) Continue working on your salvation, daily. Study the Word, pray, fast (if needed) and walk in obedience and repentance. Your first day with the Lord has been the beginning. Now, it is time to grow into a mature woman of God.

"So you ought to have deposited my money with the bankers, and at my coming I would have received back my own with interest." (Matthew 25:27) When we walk daily in using the only talent entrusted to us, we bring the Lord interest or more fruit than we can imagine. For everywhere we go, we show His light. "Let your light so shine before men, that they may see your good works and glorify your Father in heaven." (Matthew 5:16) Your true Christian living is going to do more work for Him than you can imagine. Oh, if all Christians truly walked the things they talk. This world would have been different, and how much more glory each Christian would of brought to the Lord just by observing their own salvation. Many are so deceived. Their deception not only condemns them, but also brings much blasphemy to the name of Jesus. Christianity does not justify sin, how did we get to the kind of living we live now? It is time to change and bring great glory to the Lord. When we are faithful with this one talent, God can give us more talents to use, for: "He who is faithful in what is least is faithful also in much; and he who is unjust in what is least is unjust also in much." (Luke 16:10)

"Therefore, since a promise remains of entering His rest, let us fear lest any of you seem to have come short of it." (Hebrews 4:1) While there is still time, let us work on our salvation just like an ant during the summer, while time is good. By living out our salvation on a daily basis, we can show the way of the Lord to others. Also, let's not slumber and do everything we can now while the season is still good. Let's start building our house so it will stand when the time of testing comes. At the time of David's testing, he has said the following, "Now in my prosperity I said, I shall never be moved. LORD, by Your favor You have made my mountain stand strong; You hid Your face, and I was troubled." (Psalm 30:6, 7) When things are good we do not think of bad things. When it is summer, we do not think of extreme temperatures of winter. But from the ant we should learn, that we need to prepare for the days ahead. Things are getting to the end, and our building and faith is going to be tested. It is time to pray for now and the future. It is time to analyze our spiritual walk. It is time to study His Word. It is time to gather enough strength through prayer, fasting and study of the Word, in order to endure what is ahead.

Let's also take responsibility for the things God entrusted us with. For all of us are planted in our gardens by the Lord for a reason. It is wise to ask God to show us where He wants us to be useful. If we have children, there is much work to be done. For they are our other talents. Let's analyze the way we parent. Let's ask for wisdom, ability and strength to parent them. Also, let's pray for them, teach them Scripture, and bless them daily. Let's take them to church each time we go and include them in most of our church activities.

For a wife, God has given you one more responsibility: to be your husband's helpmeet. Ask the Lord for wisdom and ability to be a godly wife. She needs to pray for her husband daily, and to remember to respect him and allow him to lead and make decisions.

While it is still the good season, there is much to be done. Many things need to be corrected. For time is closing. Very little time is left. We need not rest on the enjoyment of flowers like the butterfly, but finish up with the last preparations. For there were ten virgins, and only five entered the wedding quarters. May we and our loved ones enter, too.

II

❖ *The rock badgers are a feeble folk, yet they make their homes in the crags:*

A psalmist has said the following: "He only is my rock and my salvation; He is my defense; I shall not be moved. In God is my salvation and my glory; the rock of my strength, and my refuge, is in God." (Psalm 62:6, 7) Rock badgers are mountain rodents or mice without tales. They are just like mice – feeble and unprotected. But they are called wise in the Scripture, for they make their homes in crags (mountains or rocky high places). They run into them at a moment of danger. Jesus is our rock and cornerstone: "Behold, I lay in Zion a chief cornerstone, elect, precious, and he who believes on Him will by no means be put to shame.'" (1 Peter 2:7)

We need to be very close to Him for if we drift away, we may be in danger. The closer we are to Him the safer we are. Disobedience and sin separate us from Him. Staying away from prayer, Bible study, and visiting church on a regular basis, can drift us dangerously away, too. Daily time in the Word and prayer, is going to get us closer and closer to Him each day. One drifts away, slowly. One gets closer, slowly. None of them happen overnight.

Jesus said very powerful words, "For wherever the carcass is, there the eagles will be gathered together." (Matthew 24:28) We monthly eat His flesh and drink His blood. Jesus is our live carcass. "He gives power to the weak, and those who have no might He increases strength. Even the youths shall faint and be weary, and the young men shall utterly fall, but those who wait on the LORD shall renew their strength; <u>they shall mount up with wings like eagles</u>, they shall run and not be weary, they shall walk and not faint." (Isaiah 40:29-31) Eagles are those who rely on the strength of the One who gives strength. We need to hold on to the only 'live carcass' which is in heaven, this way we will be where He is! "For where your treasure is, there your heart will be also." (Luke 12:34) So, lets learn from the rock badgers, it is safe to make a home in the mountain of Jesus Christ!

❖ *The locusts have no king, yet they all advance in ranks:*

Why does God make an example of these insects here? Aren't they creatures of destruction and a sure sign of the wrath of God and His judgment? What is it that the Lord wants us to learn from them?

Locust is nothing more than a grasshopper. When it is alone, it is insignificant and brings no point of concern. It is when those individuals gather into a group, they become extremely powerful. "Though one may be overpowered by another, two can withstand him. And a threefold cord is not quickly broken." (Ecclesiastes 4:12) Two things we can learn from the locusts: they like to gather together and wait for the wind.

1) *Gathering together or unity:* Mark leaves us the following account: "Now John answered Him, saying, "Teacher, we saw someone who does not follow us casting out demons in Your name, and we forbade him because he does not follow us." But Jesus said, "Do not forbid him, for no one who works a miracle in My name can soon afterward speak evil of

Me. For he who is not against us is on our side. For whoever gives you a cup of water to drink in My name, because you belong to Christ, assuredly, I say to you, he will by no means lose his reward." (Mark 9:38-41) As Christian women, we need to have unity among each other. We do not need to agree on everything, nor do we need to pull each other from one church or denomination to other. Jesus name is enough for us to respect each other. The body of Christ is going to be made up of people from all nations and all denominations. He seeks those who are obedient to His Word and conform themselves to His likeness. There is much work to be done and many souls to be saved. This goal should be enough to unite us.

"Again I say to you that of two of you agree on earth concerning anything that they ask, it will be done for them by My Father in heaven. For where two or three are gathered together in My name, I am there in the midst of them." (Matthew 18:19-20) We can bring much fruit when we pray together.

2) ***Wait for the wind:*** "Therefore David inquired of the LORD, and He said, "You shall not go up; circle around behind them, and come upon them in front of the mulberry trees. And it shall be, <u>when you hear the sound of marching in the tops of mulberry trees</u>, then you shall advance quickly. For then the LORD will go out before you to strike the camp of the Philistines." And David did so, as the LORD commanded him; and he drove back the Philistines from Geba as far as Gezer." (2 Samuel 5:23-25)

Locusts need wind in order to move. They gather together in big groups and wait for the wind to carry them. Their wings do not fly long distances. They fly with the direction of the wind. Just as locusts, we need to gather in unity and same cause. Each woman at her own house, praying and filling up her cups on behalf of herself, her children, her husbands, her relatives and all the other people God is going to give her a burden for. Also, praying for repentance for her city (and/or state and country).

Before the Lord sends His fire on an alter, there must be a sacrifice, "Then the fire of the LORD fell and consumed the burnt sacrifice, and the wood and the stones and the dust, and it licked up the water that was in trench." (1 Kings 18:38) God commands women to cry out to Him in fasting, prayer and repentance, ""Now, therefore," says the LORD, "turn to Me with all your heart, with fasting, with weeping, and with mourning." So rend your heart, and not your garments; return to the LORD your God, for He is gracious and merciful, slow to anger, and of great kindness; and He relents from doing harm. Who knows if He will turn and relent, and leave a blessing behind Him – a grain offering and a drink offering for the LORD your God? Blow the trumpet in Zion, consecrate a fast, call a sacred assembly; gather the people, sanctify the congregation, assemble the elders, gather the children and nursing babes; let the bridegroom go out from his chamber, and the bride from her dressing room." (Joel 2:12-16) Also, it is time to bring forth the petitions and prayers before the Lord for our loved ones and children, once the cups are full and sacrifices of our prayers are on the alter, He will come and move. He will do what we can't, He will refresh us, and save us and our loved ones, also. We can't, but He can. We are weak but He is strong. But we must do our part, first.

We have already learned that we have very little time left. The next event is going to be the rapture. Most of us are not ready for either early or postponed rapture. It is a great possibility that most of us are going to face persecution. It is going to get worse and worse here on earth, for the birth pains are only increasing as it get closer. Our many loved ones including children and husbands are not ready either. We are in a very devastating condition and only God can help us to overcome what is ahead of us and prepare us for the rapture. This is exactly where women come into place in the following verses: "The LORD raises His voice in the presence of <u>His army</u>. His camp is <u>very large</u>; those who carry out His command are <u>powerful</u>. Indeed, the Day of the LORD is terrible and dreadful, who can endure it? The Lord gives the command; the women who proclaim the good tidings are a great host: kings of armies flee, they flee, and she who remains at home will divide the spoil! When you lie down among the sheepfolds, you are like the wings of a dove covered with silver, and its pinions with glistening gold. When the Almighty scattered the kings there, it was snowing in Zalmon." (Joel 2:11 HCSB & Psalm 68:11-14 NASB)

❖ *The spider skillfully grasps with its hands, and it is in kings' palaces:*

We all can relate to house spiders in our rooms. They seem to come from nowhere and disappear in the same manner. I seldom find them on their webs. But I find their web everywhere as an indication of their presence in my house.

These house spiders are no exception in the kings' palaces and presidential suits. No matter how much and how good the housekeeping is done. The webs find their way even where kings reside.

These creatures find admiration with God to illustrate a point. Nothing can steal the determination of a person who wants to be where one needs to be. If one wants to be with the King of kings, one is going to find a way. If one wants to see their loved ones in the same place, one is going to do everything for them to be there. One just needs the persistent determination to hold on to the King and do everything it takes to make it to His home.

It takes a skill and persistence to make a web. It is going to take us more than a wish to be in heaven. We need to be able to do everything it takes to be saved, we can't give up. For giving up means being in a place of condemnation and away from the King of kings. For Jesus Himself has said the following: "He who has an ear, let him hear what the Spirit says to the churches. <u>To him who overcomes</u> I will give to eat from the tree of life, which is in the midst of the Paradise of God. And behold, I am coming quickly and My reward is with Me, to give to every one according to his work. I am the Alpha and the Omega, the Beginning and the End, the First and the Last. Blessed are those who do His commandments, that they may have the right to the tree of life, and may enter through the gates into the city. But outside are dogs and sorcerers and sexually immoral and murderers and idolaters, and whoever loves and practices a lie." (Revelation 2:7 & 22:12-15)

There is much to overcome yet. For, "the end of all things is at hand; therefore be serious and watchful in your prayers." (1 Peter 4:7) We can do it only with God's help, just as Paul has done, "I can do all things through Christ who strengthens me." (Philippians 4:13)

III

"Thus saith the LORD, what iniquity have your fathers found in me, that they are gone far from me, and have walked after vanity, and are become vain? Rise up, you women who are at ease, hear my voice; you complacent daughters, give ear to my speech. In a year and some days you will be troubled, you complacent women; for the vintage will fail, the gathering will not come. Tremble, you women who are at ease; be troubled, you complacent ones; strip yourselves bare, and gird sackcloth on your waist. Because you have forgotten the God of your salvation, and have not been mindful of the Rock of your stronghold, therefore you will plant pleasant plants and set out foreign seedlings; in the day you will make your plant to grow, and in the morning you will make your seed to flourish; but the harvest will be a heap of ruins in the day of grief and desperate sorrow." (Jeremiah 2:5 KJV, Isaiah 32:9-11 & 17:10, 11)

It is time to learn from Mary and Martha to make the right priorities in life, "And Jesus answered and said to her, "Martha, Martha, you are worried and troubled about many things. <u>But one thing is needed, and Mary has chosen that good part, which will not be taken away from her."</u>" (Luke 10:41, 42) Let's seek for what is eternal, so we can reap salvation: "Do not be deceived, God is not mocked; for whatever a man sows, that he will also reap. For he who sows to his flesh will of the flesh reap corruption, but he who sows to the Spirit will of the Spirit reap everlasting life. And let us not grow weary while doing good, for in due season we shall reap if we do not lose heart." (Galatians 6:7-9) "So don't worry, saying, 'What will we eat?' or 'What will we drink?' or 'What will we wear?' For the idolaters eagerly seek all these things, and your heavenly Father knows that you need them. <u>But seek first the kingdom of God and His righteousness, and all these things will be provided for you.</u> Therefore don't worry about tomorrow, because tomorrow will worry about itself. Each day has enough trouble of its own." (Matthew 6:31-34 HCSB) Let us put eternal things first and analyze everything we do. For many things we worry about at this time are worthless in the test of eternity.

What is our faith producing? What do we plant? Let's learn from the ants, rock badgers, locusts and a spider:

- The ants – to prepare now for the things ahead.
- The rock badgers – to make ourselves closer to our Rock and take safety in Him alone.
- The locusts – to unite in common goal and prayer and wait for Holy Spirit to move.
- The spider's skill – to do anything it takes to be in the King's palace.

Let us seek the truth while there is summer and still time. Let us come to our Rock and truly ask Him in the persistent prayer to show us the way, open our eyes, set us free of any deception and ask Him to not lose us, our husbands, our children, and our loved ones. The door is very narrow and a few can find it. Are you and your family among those few? For only three were saved from Sodom and eight during the flood. Let us bring protection for the cold months. Let it be true of us the following: "She is not afraid of snow for her household, for all her household is clothed with scarlet. Charm is deceitful and beauty is passing, but a woman who fears the LORD, she shall be praised. Give her of the fruit of her hands, and let her own works praise her in the gates." (Proverbs 31:21, 30, 31) Let us not just make noise, but truly carry in our hands the fruit of our labor. Let's not be deceived by the people who are servants of the enemy of our souls. For the multitude in hell including those who thought of themselves as Christians. May our faith be not in vain. May it indeed bring us to our set destination. Let us come to God Himself and take responsibility for the salvation of our souls into our hands and hand them over to the Lord in our prayers.

IV

I have combined several verses from the Bible to illustrate the importance of our call and show God's heart for the time we live: *"'As I live!' declares the Lord God, 'I take no pleasure in the death of the wicked, but rather that the wicked turn from his way and live.' For God so loved the world, that He gave His only begotten Son, that whoever believes in Him shall not perish, but have eternal life. For God did not send His Son into the world to judge the world, but that the world might be saved through Him. The Spirit of the Lord is upon the Son, because He anointed the Son to preach the gospel to the poor. He has sent the Son to proclaim release to the captives, and recovery of sight to the blind, to set free those who are oppressed. To proclaim the favorable year of the Lord. God does not show partiality.*

The Lord is not slow about His promise, as some count slowness, but is patient toward men, not wishing for any to perish but for all to come to repentance. Therefore beseech the Lord of the harvest to send out workers into His harvest. Therefore, let all supplications, prayers, intercessions, and giving of thanks be made for all men, for kings and all who are in authority, that we may lead a quiet and peaceable life in all godliness and reverence. For this is good and acceptable in the sight of God our Savior, who desires all men to be saved and to come to the knowledge of the truth. For there is one God and one Mediator between God and men, the Man Christ Jesus, who gave Himself a ransom for all.

And the cry is being heard already: 'Behold, the bridegroom is coming; go out to meet him!' We need to do homage to the Son, that He not become angry, and we perish in the way, for His wrath may soon be kindled. But the Lord desires mercy, and not sacrifice, for He did not come to call the righteous, but sinners, to repentance. God has no pleasure in the death of a sinner. This is why Jesus has come: to preach the gospel to the poor; to heal the brokenhearted, to proclaim liberty to the captives and recovery of sight to the blind, to set at liberty those who are oppressed; to proclaim the acceptable year of the Lord.

Assuredly, Jesus has said to us, "Whatever you bind on earth will be bound in heaven, and whatever you loose on earth will be loose in heaven." Therefore, we need to deliver those who are drawn toward death, and hold back those stumbling to the slaughter. Can we say, "Surely we did not know this?" Does not He who weighs the hearts consider it? He who keeps your soul, does He not know it? And will He not render to each man according to his deeds? God has given us the sword of the Spirit, which is the Word of God. We need to use the Word of God in our prayers. For the weapons of our warfare are not carnal but mighty in God for pulling down strongholds, casting down arguments and every high thing that exalts itself against the knowledge of God, bringing every thought into captivity to the obedience of Christ.

Jesus has said to us, "To go into all the world and preach the gospel to every creature." Many have hid their talents in the ground. Let's obey the Lord by liberating the captives and the oppressed through our prayers. The effective, fervent prayer of a righteous man avails much. Assuredly, Jesus has said to us, "whatever we bind on earth will be bound in heaven, and whatever we loose on earth will be loose in heaven. And if two of us agree on earth concerning anything that we ask, it will be done for us by our Father in heaven. For where two or three are gathered together in His name, He is there in the midst of them." And whatever we ask we receive from Him, because we keep His commandments and do those things that are pleasing in His sight.

The instant God speaks concerning a nation and concerning a kingdom, to pluck up, to pull down, and to destroy it, if that nation against whom God has spoken turns from its evil, He will relent of the disaster that He thought to bring upon it. When God shuts up heaven and there is no rain, or commands the locust to devour the land, or sends pestilence among His people, if His people who are called by His name will humble themselves, and pray and seek His face, and turn from their wicked ways, then He will hear from heaven, and will forgive their sin and heal their land. When Daniel prayed to God with sackcloth, fasting and supplication and repenting of his nation's sins, God has heard him.

For the Lord utters His voice before His army; surely His camp is very great, for strong is he who carries out His word. The day of the Lord is indeed great and very awesome, and who can endure it? "Yet even now," declares the Lord, "Return to Me with all your heart, and with fasting, weeping and mourning; and rend your heart and not your garments." Now return to the Lord your God, for He is gracious and compassionate, slow to anger, abounding in lovingkindness and relenting of evil.

God needs prayers worriers, therefore the Lord raises His voice in the presence of His army and gives a command; the women who carry out His command are powerful, they are a great host and make a very large camp. Because of their obedience, they will delight in the Almighty and lift their faces to God. They will pray to Him and He will hear them and He will rescue many by the purity of their hands."' (all (with slight modification to show the point) from either NKJV, HCSB, NASB: Ezekiel 33:11b; John 3:16, 17; Luke 4:18, 19; Acts 10:34b; 2 Peter 3:9; Matthew 9:38; 25:6a, 24-30, 9:13, 18:18-20; 1 Timothy 2:1-6a; Psalm 2:12; Proverbs 24:11, 12; Ephesians 6:17; 2 Corinthians 10:4, 5; Mark 16:15; James 5:16b; 1 John 3:22; Jeremy 18:7, 8; 2 Chronicles 7:13-14; Joel 2:11-13, & (Jam of Joel 2:11, Psalm 68:11-14 & Job 22:26-30)

V

Are we in God's army? We should earnestly start seeking God for our family and He is going to show us more. Time is running out. The darkness gets thicker and thicker. It only means that those who put their trust in the Lord can see where to go. It is not easy to enter through the narrow gate, but with God we can.

As of Ephesians 6:18 we are to be watchful with all perseverance for all saints in prayer. We are all the body of Christ, therefore we need to pray for each other. We can't pray for everyone, nor should we. But we should seek from the Lord who we really need to pray for. Apostle Paul needed prayers. We are often in need of others' prayers. We should pray for our pastor and other leadership in the church. Also, those who really need our prayers. Gospel preachers, just like Apostle Paul are in great need of our praying support. Once we engage in daily prayers, we are going to discern for who to pray. Also, we would know for how long to pray. Praying for others can heal and bring blessings, but it needs to be tailored to the individual's strength. We need to realize how much we have on our list and how we pray. For every prayer is a battle. Once we embrace our prayer work, God is going to teach us more about prayer.

I have been leading a praying life for several years. Some people call me a prayer warrior, perhaps... But I do not consider it so.

I was drawn into this activity after series of personal trials. I have learned many things and most importantly the power of praying. I realized myself how much I needed someone to pray for me in the right way. Also, I realized how much easier I could persevere when someone stood in the prayer gap for me. Then, I realized that I can no longer allow my life and my loved ones lives to chance. We are in a serious battle. We need to constantly persevere for self, loved ones and others. I have had wonderful spiritual blessings since I embraced my prayer life. Taking a reasonable load of burdens for other believers has given me a new meaning. I receive protection for self while praying for others. For God blesses and protects those who care and pray for others. Also, when the church actively prays for each other, it receives special protection. It is like caring for a body. Everyone cares for each member of the body through prayer.

Besides, praying for my immediate family, I pray for my Christian and non-Christian relatives. My list also consist of the people who God personally puts on my heart. These people usually Christians, but there are some who are not. When certain persons come to my mind often, I know, God wants me to pray for them. Usually, those are the people who have been forgotten by many and barely make it by.

If we could just pray daily, the Scriptures I have listed below, only for ourselves and our immediate family, the Lord will work towards saving us and them. If all Christians prayed this way, there wouldn't be any Christians and their immediate families in hell. Think of the difference we would make in the eyes of eternity, if all Christians prayed for their believing and unbelieving extended families or relatives. Now, what if we all have been praying for each other? What if we all prayed the following prayer: 'Lord of the harvest, please send out laborers into Your harvest?' How about daily blessings for our government, ordinance of man including police? How about asking wisdom on their behalf to run and pass the laws? How about uniting in some serious petitions for many things and people? How about praying for all our pastors, ministers, preachers, missionaries, and persecuted church? They all exist. They need our prayers daily, for they are being attacked the most.

We really shouldn't ask why this or that is happening, if we slack off in our prayers. Things have gotten very bad. Our government has passed bad laws. Christians go to hell by millions, for they failed to pray, obey God and have lost the fight, or have been deceived. What about the rest of the world? When are we going to wake up? Things are going to get only worse. But this worse can be better if we all unite in prayer. May it never be on our post, that one of our children has slipped away to hell. Never! Never! May it never be that we've set in front of the TV or a magazine and slipped away there, too. May we fight if not for others, at least fight for ourselves and our children. Wake up, wake up, church! Wake up women! We can't pray for all but we can pray daily for something and someone. At least, bring petitions on the alter for ourselves and our families. Let the Lord enjoy the fragrance of your sacrifice and send His fire on it to burn it. If there is no sacrifice, there is nothing for fire to burn. Fire doesn't come on an empty alter.

In order to be saved, we need to come to Christ Himself and seek Him for ourselves and family in prayer and fasting while there is still time for it. Time is coming short, we need to hurry. It is time to develop a personal Bible reading and studying time with prayer. If we can't seem to succeed in finding time for it, we can ask God to help us. We need to be honest with Him that we can't and ask Him to help us. Let's analyze our day, where does our time go? Perhaps we can cancel some of our activities? We do not need to be involved in anything at all if those things come in the way of our time with God and therefore our salvation. How much TV do we watch? How much time do we spend on a computer or a phone with our friends? It is possible to be without those popular social networks. Computer games shouldn't even be a mention, here. TV?

Well, the kind of things they produce there, shouldn't be watched neither by us nor our children. How can we drink abominable things and expect God to be pleased with us? What about books? Should any book really take time from the BOOK? Well, once we begin seeking God, He will purge us and our families of many things. It is not going to happen overnight but it will happen. We are going to look at things in a different light. It is sad that we drink dirty water and get involved in things that are hateful to God. But this is why we are seeking Him now, so we will not be condemned forever with the abominable. We are so fallen and so far away from perfection, that we cannot save ourselves. God is our only option. We must start seeking Him on our knees, daily.

It is important to have our prayers meaningful and result producing. Many of us come to a prayer with no idea how to pray and what to pray about. Therefore, one needs to sit down and make a prayer list or prayer petitions. Personally, I pray for forty day intervals. I try to be consistent with my prayer and pray daily. There are days when I miss, because life happens, and with all my effort I could not get to this special petition or intercessory prayer. For each day I pray, I draw a tally mark, until I get forty marks. At the end of the forty days, I analyze my list. I eliminate what is no longer needed, keep the ones I need to continue to pray for and add more. I allow God to pounder on my heart what to pray about. During the forty day period, I sometimes drop the petitions or add more. The goal is to bring the same petitions for a reasonable amount of time for cups to be filled with prayers to be answered and have some kind of sacrifice on my prayer alter for the Lord to start working to produce results.

Do not think that you need to save the world. Start small and specific. Your greatest concern is yourself, your children and your husband, then relatives, friends and church members. Each time you engage in any petition you put a burden or load on yourself. It must be just right and not overloaded. Know how much you can carry. For some, praying for the immediate family is a load just enough to carry. Others can pray and fast for more. More serious petitions need to be done in united agreement between a group of several people.

Circle yourself and your family, especially your children from all evil and ask for God's mercy. Things are going to get worse, those who fill up the protection cup in prayers are going to be better off than the others. Pray for your children and don't leave them to chance, for satan has prepared many snares for them now, and many dangers as the days approach closer to the end. There is a huge spiritual warfare for every single soul, do not allow the enemy to cast a lot on any of your children. The easy access to cell phones has made children exposed to pornography. Many video games and TV expose children to violence. Many cartoons are not healthy for our children either. The devil seeks anyone he can devour, he doesn't forget about our children, either. He finds ways to steal their innocence and make them unclean. The time has come when we need to be extra vigilant of our children. Also, teach children to pray short prayers of repentance, daily: 'Jesus, please forgive me for (any sin) I may have done today. Keep me safe and help me to be obedient to my parents. Thank you for dying for me and loving me. Amen.'

VI

❖ *What to pray about?*

1. Things that are of eternal value are more important than earthly value. For example, it is OK to pray for your son's right choice of college, but it may be wiser to ask God to do His will in your son's choosing. For some colleges often do more harm than good for our souls.
2. Be specific in your petitions, but do not tell God to do something in a certain way. Also, your petitions must always be for the benefit of a person. Never ask for something you wouldn't like to receive yourself. Don't ask

for a punishment or a teaching lesson, etc. For example, one mother in her prayers for her prodigal son has been asking God to send him a wilderness in order for her son to come to God. The poor young man has gotten the wilderness she has asked, but the son didn't repent and both her and her son have gone through unnecessary turmoil. Later, she repented of it. Now, she prays just for the Lord to bring her son to repentance and salvation.

3. Ask for answers to certain Biblical questions or truths. For example, ask God to reveal to you His truth about baptism of the Holy Spirit?

4. Ask Him to make the Word of God real to you and to have understanding of it. Ask Him to do everything it takes to save you and your loved ones.

5. Always surround yourself and your loved ones with a circle of protection in everything for now and in the future.

6. Use Scripture and your own words.

7. Do not forget to give Him praise and glory, pray in Spirit (or tongues), bring your daily repentance in. Most of all, remember to be patient and know that God listens when you come in sincerity. God is not partial, "In truth I perceive that God shows no partiality. But in every nation whoever fears Him and works righteousness is accepted by Him." (Acts 10:34b-35)

8. Remember to talk to Him like to your friend and Daddy.

9. Pray for other saints or believers and the persecuted church.

10. Pray for ordinance of men.

11. Pray for peace of Jerusalem and safety of the people of Israel. (This particular area brings blessing into one's life.)

12. Use the Lord's prayer daily. It is very powerful for our protection and growth. Also, when under attack, pray the Psalm 91 and/or the Lord's Prayer.

▪ ***Here are the basic daily petition prayers:*** Scripture praying is a most powerful weapon. Scripture praying produces more powerful results and allow us to pray the way we can't, it nails exactly the way it should be, because it is the Word of God. These prayers are mostly personal and concentrate on immediate family with no strenuous requests. If petitioned daily, it is going to produce positive spiritual growth and protection for the whole family. Feel free to modify to your needs and liking. Add your daily needs and petitions, etc. (These prayers can be used for your pastor, church leaders, gospel preachers, missionaries, church members, etc., too. When praying for others, take on only as much you can carry.) If every Christian woman prays on a daily basis these verses, and adds other petitions and verses for her family needs, the result will be catastrophic to the kingdom of darkness in the locust's proportions.

'Lord, be the wall of fire all around (names), and reveal Your glory in (their) midst.' Based on Zechariah 2:5

'May the Lord bless (names) and keep (them); the Lord make His face shine on (them), and be gracious to (them); the Lord lift up His countenance on (them), and give (them) peace.' Based on Numbers 6:23-27

'God grant (names), according to the riches of His glory, to be strengthened with the power through His Spirit in the inner man; so that Christ may dwell in (their) heart through faith; and that (they), being rooted and grounded in love, may be able to comprehend with all the saints what is breadth and length and depth, and to know the love of Christ which surpasses knowledge, that (they) may be filled up to all the fullness of God.' Based on Ephesians 3:16-19

'Let (names) be born again and enter through the small gate and walk the narrow road so (they) be saved, find life and enter the kingdom of heaven.' Based on John 3:3 & Matthew 7:13, 14

'Heavenly Father, I pray in the name of Jesus, may (names) love abound still more and more in knowledge and all discernment, that (they) may approve the things that are excellent, that (they) may be sincere and without offense till the day of Christ, being filled with the fruits of righteousness which are by Jesus Christ, to the glory and praise of God.' Based on Philippians 1:9-11

'Jesus, please help (names) to abide in Your Word and keep Your Word, so (names) shall never see death, know the truth and be set free.' Based on John 8:51, 31, 32

'Lord Jesus, please help (names) to endure to the end and overcome in order to be saved and eat from the tree of life.' Based on Revelation 2:7

'Work in (names) to will and to do everything to Your good pleasure.' Based on Philippians 2:13

'Help (names) to think on these things: whatsoever things are just, whatsoever things are pure, whatsoever things are lovely, whatsoever things are of good report, if there be any virtue and praise.' Based on Philippians 4:8

'Lord, please deliver (names) from every evil work, and preserve unto Your heavenly kingdom: to You be glory for ever and ever.' Based on 2 Timothy 4:18

'Let the words of (names) mouth and the meditations of (their) heart be acceptable in Your sight, O Lord, (their) strength and Redeemer.' Based on Psalms 19:14

Here are some other ones, too: Isaiah 54:13, Matthew 22:37-39, Ephesians 1:17-18, Galatians 5:22, 23, James 3:17, Psalm 25:4-7, 16-22; 23:1-4 and many more.

VII

The prayers below are more strenuous, but they are much needed and will bring much fruit for the Lord. They are for women who want to lead the work in prayer and be prayer worriers. Unity in these prayers is going to produce the locust's devastation to the kingdom of darkness. Feel free to use all of them or pick and choose. Please, pray them daily or on indicated days so we may unite in prayer.

- **Prayer for support of women who work in mission fields:** It is tough out there for both men and women. But women have the grater enmity from the snake. Therefore, let's daily keep our sisters in prayer support for they labor for the Lord's glory and His kingdom. Feel free to include male missionaries and their families as well. Pray it daily, or at least every *Monday*.

'Lord, be the wall of fire around women missionaries around the world, may You be glorified in their midst and through their work. Help them to proclaim Your truth with boldness and perseverance. Give them strength to continue their endeavor, support them in their spiritual and physical needs. Deliver them from unreasonable and wicked men. Lord, please deliver them from every evil work, and preserve unto Your heavenly kingdom: to You be glory for ever and ever. Amen.'

- ***Prayer for the persecuted church:*** Please, pray it daily or at least on *Tuesdays*.

'Lord, for the sake of Your Son, be the wall of fire around all persecuted Christians around the world, especially in Muslim believing countries and North Korea, and be glorified in their midst. Help them to be strong, patient and faithful. Show them mercy and Your divine protection and intervention. Ease their suffering and give them endurance. Have mercy on their children and their souls. Let their persecutors come to repentance, for the

Savior desires all men to be saved. May this persecution ignite the spread of the Gospel and adding more souls to Your kingdom. Amen.'

- **Prayer for those who have been human trafficked and is used in sex trade:** This is a much needed prayer and based on Psalm 72:12-14. It is cruel to ignore the pain and helplessness of all women involved in this trade including infants and children. If all women would pray this prayer at least once a week, God can deliver and prevent many victims. Remember, evil can progress only when there is no opposition. I call all my readers to pray this prayer at least every *Wednesday*. We are powerful together!

'Lord God, in the name of Jesus, we pray for all those women and children who are being human trafficked and in sex slavery, please deliver them, help them, heal them and save their souls from eternal condemnation. For You deliver the needy when they cry, the poor also, and those who have no helper. You spare the poor and needy, and save the souls of the needy. You redeem their life from oppression and violence. Amen.'

- **Prayer for our men:** For we need them to rise up and become who they ought to be, the strong leaders of our churches, bold proclaimers of the Gospel, and standing up for the truth. Pray it daily or every *Thursday*.

'Lord God, in the name of Jesus, please rise up our sons, husbands, brothers, and uncles to be the mighty men of God. Give us Daniels, Peters, Pauls, Jameses, Johns, and Barnabuses. May they proclaim Your truth with boldness and power. Amen.'

- ***This prayer can change the atmosphere in your town and raise prayer warriors:*** It is based on the 1 Timothy chapter 2. Please pray it daily or every *Friday*.

'Lord, in the name of Jesus, please raise up people who can be prayer warriors and pray for the benefit and salvation of many. Thank you for all the residents, rulers, and people in authority, including police of (town, county, city, state). Please, bless them and give them ability and wisdom to pass the laws and govern, so we may lead a quiet and peaceable life in all godliness and reverence. For this is good and acceptable in the sight of God our Savior, who desires all men to be saved and come to the knowledge of the truth. Lord of the harvest, please send out laborers into Your harvest. Amen.'

- **This is a sample of a simple prayer in time of a disaster:** It is always safe to pray for the safety of the church and spreading of the Gospel during a disaster. Pray it daily, or at least every <u>Saturday</u>.

'Lord, please be the wall of fire all around Christians in Nepal and other areas of unrest. Protect them from any harm and human trafficking. May your kingdom advance and the earthquake in Nepal be the vehicle for saving a multitude of souls. May doors in Nepal be open to receive your true Gospel. Lord of the harvest, please send out laborers into Your harvest in Nepal and other areas of unrest. Amen.'

- **Here is the revival prayer that is going to make a big difference for the kingdom of God.** Please, pray this in unity either with your church praying group or private women's praying group. I do not recommend to take this prayer on individually. This prayer is going to untie people to be able to receive the gospel into salvation. This prayer can allow God to mightily move and intercede on behalf of many people and their internal salvation. This prayer can produce revivals. Its' effectiveness is going to be measured by the number of days it is being petitioned. For this is going to produce a battle within the spiritual realms. I believe that it is going to be needed at least forty days for the petition to start producing the necessary results. After forty days eliminate the confession and repentance of sins and continue with the rest of the petition. If forty days can't be prayed, do any amount of days you can: three, seven, ten, twelve, twenty one, or thirty. It is better to pray at least a few days, than none at all. This prayer is based on Daniel's prayer upon completion of seventy years of Jewish exile to Babylon, 1st Timothy 2, and 2nd Chronicles 7. I have modified this prayer for our days and based on what the Lord has revealed and impressed on me through years of personal prayers and Bible study.

"When I shut up heaven and there is no rain, or command the locusts to devour the land, or send pestilence among My people, if My people who are called by My name will humble themselves, and pray and seek My face, and turn from their wicked ways, then I will hear from heaven, and will forgive their sin and heal their land." (2 Chronicles 7:13, 14)

'Our Heavenly Father, in the name of Your Son, Jesus Christ, hear this prayer of our petition before Your face. We repent for the sins of people in our (town, city, county, or state) and ask for Your mercy, forgiveness and salvation because of Your name and Your glory. We are aware that the people have sinned against You and Your laws and Your commandments. We repent for all the sins which have been committed by (town, city, county, or state): fornication, adultery, homosexuality, all sorts of sexual abominations, pornography, divorces, all kind of human trafficking and abuse, extortions, murders, abortions, hatred, jealousies, envy, covetousness, love of money, revelry, contentions, drunkenness, smoking, drug use, idolatry, uncleanness, lewdness, sorcery, outbursts of wrath, evil speech, and all kind of abomination and unrighteousness in Your sight.

Also, we repent for the sins of our church, for we have sinned, and have committed iniquity, and have done wickedly, and have rebelled by departing from Your precepts and from Your judgements, from Your Word and from Your commandments. We have forgotten to be your bondservants and went after our own follies and each our own ways. We repent for allowing in our midst all sorts of sexual immorality, divorces, partiality, hypocrisy, all sort of uncleanness, extortions, murders, abortions, hatred, jealousies, envy, covetousness, love of money, revelry, contentions, drunkenness, smoking, outbursts of wrath, gossip and evil speech. We repent for our spiritual laziness for forgetting to be the salt and the light of the world, and for using other sources for studying Your Word and putting aside our true source of the truth – Your Holy Bible. We repent for allowing false doctrines to enter in our midst. We repent for rejecting the Holy Spirit and doing everything on our own. We repent that on our post many souls are slipping away into hell while we are busy following and proving our agendas. We repent for not fasting and praying for the lost.

We thank You for Your Son's blood and His redeeming sacrifice. We thank You for by Your mercy we haven't been destroyed yet. We thank You for Your Holy Word and the work of the Holy Spirit. We thank You for the physical blessings You have been pouring out on our country. We thank you for Your providence with food, clean water, clothing, shelter, and peace. We give thanks for all men and rulers of (town, city, county, or state), bless them and help them to seek You and pass moral laws, so that we may lead a quiet and peaceable life in all godliness and reverence. Lord of the harvest, please send out laborers into Your harvest and in our churches, schools, higher education institutions, nursing homes, hospitals, and our homes, for this is good and acceptable in the sight of God our Savior, for You desire all men to be saved and to come to knowledge of the truth. For Christ Jesus is the only one God and one Mediator between God and men, who gave Himself a ransom for all.

We realize, that we are weak but You are strong, we are fallen and without You we can do nothing. We humbly ask You to hear our prayer and supplication and answer us because of Your Son's sacrifice and Your mercy. Please, forgive us and pour out Your Spirit and move Your way amongst us for salvation of many. Give us unity, strength to persevere, faith, and ability and willingness to serve You with no compromises, prayer and fasting. Amen.'

VIII

As we get closer to the Lord through prayer and Bible study, He is going to use us in more ways than just prayer. Be prepared to listen to Him and act as He directs. He likes us to be faithful in small things and use us in small daily tasks and interactions where we are being planted. God is looking for servants who are willing to be used in reaching out people who cannot be reached through regular means. He plants everyone in the places He wants to produce certain outcomes for His glory and salvation of His people. God's army grows through prayer and obedience to His Word, and then produces fruit and outcomes as He deems to be useful for His glory and His purpose.

""Come here," the Philistine called to David, "and I'll give your flesh to the birds of the sky and the wild beasts!" David said to the Philistine, "You come against me with a dagger, spear, and sword, but <u>I come against you in the name of the LORD of Hosts, the God of Israel's armies</u> – you have defied Him. Today, the LORD will hand you over to me. Today, I'll strike you down, cut your head off, and give the corpses of the Philistine camp to the birds of the sky and the creatures of the earth. Then all the world will know that Israel has a God, and this whole assembly will know that <u>it is not by sword or by spear that the LORD saves</u>, for the battle is the LORD's. He will hand you over to us."" (1 Sam.17:44-47 HCSB) Who is our Goliath today? The battle is the Lord's! We can overcome our enemy only with the help and the power of God of Israel, Jesus Christ! David knew that apart from God, he has no chance with this giant. Apart from God we are weak and no match to our spiritual enemy.

David didn't just get to the battle field and stand there. He got a sling and five stones, then he used his insignificant weapons and got his way with the giant. We shouldn't expect any victory by just standing and facing our enemy, either. We have mighty tools in our hands for the spiritual warfare: whole armor of God, prayer and fasting. It is time for us to make the best use of them against this ancient snake and win! For the battle will be done by the Lord Himself as long as we use our sling and the stones! "When the Philistine started forward to attack him, David ran quickly to the battle line to meet the Philistine. David put his hand in the bag, took out a stone, slung it, and hit the Philistine on his forehead. The stone sank into his forehead, and he fell on his face to the ground. <u>David defeated the Philistine with a sling and a stone</u>. Even though David had no sword, he struck down the Philistine and killed him. David ran and stood over him. He grabbed the Philistine's sword, pulled it from its sheath, and used it to kill him. Then he cut off his head. When the Philistines saw their hero was dead, they ran." (1 Sam. 17:48-51 HCSB)

For the Lord tells us today to rise up, for He wants to do great things in the advancement of His kingdom and His glory, for salvation and deliverance of many! "Why, when I came, was there no man? Why, when I called, was there none to answer? Is My hand shortened at all that it cannot redeem? Or have I no power to deliver? Call to Me, and I will answer you, and show you great and mighty things, which you do not know." (Isaiah 50:2b & Jeremiah 33:3)

"Do you not know that those who run in a race all run, but one receives the prize? Run in such a way that you may obtain it. And everyone who competes for the prize is temperate in all things. Now they do it to obtain a perishable crown, but we for an imperishable crown. Therefore <u>I run thus</u>: not with uncertainty. <u>Thus I fight</u>: not as one who beats the air. But <u>I discipline my body</u> and <u>bring it into subjection</u>, lest, when I have preached to others, I myself should become disqualified." (1 Cor. 9:24-27) It takes discipline to finish the race. It takes discipline to pray and study the Word daily. May we not slumber and let's put aside our spiritual laziness. This world is passing and all its desires. Eternity is lasting and never ending. After our last breath, we won't care whether or not we were beautiful, skinny, fat, drove expensive vehicles, or had a big and up to date house. When we are dead, we won't care if our children have been to all the sport's practices, about their education and popularity. When we are on the other side of eternity, we will care whether or not we are in heaven and our loved ones, too.

May not the following words be true of any of us and our loved ones: "The harvest is past, the summer is ended, and we are not saved!" (Jeremiah 8:20) Therefore, "Let us search out and examine our ways, and turn back to the LORD; let us lift our hearts and hands to God in heaven." (Lamentations 3:40, 41)

> **CONCLUSION:** It is possible to do much work for the kingdom of God and change the outcome of many things for us, our families, our neighborhoods, our cities, and much of humanity through regular prayer petitions and being the salt and the light of the world. God is eager to answer prayers which are on His heart. He wants to help humanity here and save them for eternity. But He needs prayer warriors through whom He can untie the ones in bondage, make them see and hear. God's mighty army fights on their knees. Let's use the wisdom of the little four of God's creatures to save selves and others.

> **WHAT TO DO: 1.** Develop a prayer list. **2.** Start praying daily off that list. **3.** Analyze and change your lifestyle for it to be productive and glorifying to the Father. **4.** Develop your daily

Bible study and reading. **5.** Most of all don't give up and ask the Lord for the strength.

➤ **NOTE:** After this chapter, I purposely include prayers for your convenience, so you can copy and use them. Please, be sure to check my website. Once it gets running, I plan to write more prayers and other interactions. I hope to use this website to unite serious women of God to pray in unity for things that matter and produce some serious and wonderful results for the kingdom of God. Also, check out the list of 'Useful Resources' in the back of this book.

<u>www.sheshallcrushthehead.com</u>

Prayers

- **Daily Scriptural Prayers:**

'Lord, be the wall of fire all around (names), and reveal Your glory in (their) midst.' Based on Zechariah 2:5

'May the Lord bless (names) and keep (them); the Lord make His face shine on (them), and be gracious to (them); the Lord lift up His countenance on (them), and give (them) peace.' Based on Numbers 6:23-27

'God grant (names), according to the riches of His glory, to be strengthened with the power through His Spirit in the inner man; so that Christ may dwell in (their) heart through faith; and that (they), being rooted and grounded in love, may be able to comprehend with all the saints what is breadth and length and depth, and to know the love of Christ which surpasses knowledge, that (they) may be filled up to all the fullness of God.' Based on Ephesians 3:16-19

'Let (names) be born again and enter through the small gate and walk the narrow road so (they) be saved, find life and enter the kingdom of heaven.' Based on John 3:3 & Matthew 7:13, 14

'Heavenly Father, I pray in the name of Jesus, may (names) love abound still more and more in knowledge and all discernment, that (they) may approve the things that are excellent, that (they) may be sincere and without offense till the day of Christ, being

filled with the fruits of righteousness which are by Jesus Christ, to the glory and praise of God.' Based on Philippians 1:9-11

'Jesus, please help (names) to abide in Your Word and keep Your Word, so (names) shall never see death, know the truth and be set free.' Based on John 8:51, 31, 32

'Lord Jesus, please help (names) to endure to the end and overcome in order to be saved and eat from the tree of life.' Based on Revelation 2:7

'Work in (names) to will and to do everything to Your good pleasure.' Based on Philippians 2:13

'Help (names) to think on these things: whatsoever things are just, whatsoever things are pure, whatsoever things are lovely, whatsoever things are of good report, if there be any virtue and praise.' Based on Philippians 4:8

'Lord, please deliver (names) from every evil work, and preserve unto Your heavenly kingdom: to You be glory for ever and ever.' Based on 2 Timothy 4:18

'Let the words of (names) mouth and the meditations of (their) heart be acceptable in Your sight, O Lord, (their) strength and Redeemer.' Based on Psalms 19:14

- **Prayer for support of women who work in mission fields:** <u>Monday</u> or daily.

'Lord, be the wall of fire around women missionaries around the world, may You be glorified in their midst and through their work. Help them to proclaim Your truth with boldness and perseverance. Give them strength to continue their endeavor, support them in their spiritual and physical needs. Deliver them

from unreasonable and wicked men. Lord, please deliver them from every evil work, and preserve unto Your heavenly kingdom: to You be glory for ever and ever. Amen.'

- **Prayer for the persecuted church:** _Tuesdays_ or daily.

'Lord, for the sake of Your Son, be the wall of fire around all persecuted Christians around the world, especially in Muslim believing countries and North Korea, and be glorified in their midst. Help them to be strong, patient and faithful. Show them mercy and Your divine protection and intervention. Ease their suffering and give them endurance. Have mercy on their children and their souls. Let their persecutors come to repentance, for Savior desires all men to be saved. May this persecution ignite the spread of the Gospel and add more souls to Your kingdom. Amen.'

- **Prayer for those who have been caught in human trafficking and are being used in sex trade:** _Wednesday_ or daily.

'Lord God, in the name of Jesus, we pray for all those women and children who are being human trafficked and in sex slavery, please deliver them, help them, heal them and save their souls from eternal condemnation. For You deliver the needy when they cry, the poor also, and those who have no helper. You spare the poor and needy, and save the souls of the needy. You redeem their life from oppression and violence. Amen.'

- **Prayer for our men:** _Thursday_ or daily.

'Lord God, in the name of Jesus, please rise up our sons, husbands, brothers, and uncles to be the mighty men of God. Give us Daniels, Peters, Pauls, Jameses, Johns, and Barnabuses. May they proclaim Your truth with boldness and power. Amen.'

- **Prayer for your town and prayer warriors:** <u>Friday</u> or daily.

'Lord, in the name of Jesus, please raise up people who can be prayer warriors and pray for the benefit and salvation of many. Thank you for all the residents, rulers, and people in authority, including police of (town, county, city, state). Please, bless them and give them ability and wisdom to pass the laws and govern, so we may lead a quiet and peaceable life in all godliness and reverence. For this is good and acceptable in the sight of God our Savior, who desires all men to be saved and come to the knowledge of the truth. Lord of the harvest, please send out laborers into Your Harvest. Amen.'

- **Sample prayer in time of a disaster:** <u>Saturday</u> or daily.

'Lord, please be the wall of fire all around Christians in Nepal and other areas of unrest. Protect them from any harm and human trafficking. May your kingdom advance and the earthquake in Nepal be the vehicle for saving a multitude of souls. May doors in Nepal be open to receive your true Gospel. Lord of the harvest, please send out laborers into Your harvest in Nepal and other areas of unrest. Amen.'

- **Psalm 91** (with slight modification to make it as a prayer):

'I dwell in the shelter of the Most High and I will abide in the shadow of the Almighty. I will say to the Lord, "my refuge and my fortress, my God, in whom I trust!" For it is He who delivers me from the snare of the trapper, and from the deadly pestilence. He will cover me with His pinions, and under His wings I may seek refuge; His faithfulness is a shield and bulwark. I will not be afraid of the terror by night, or of arrow that flies by day; of the pestilence that stalks in darkness, or of the destruction that lays waste at noon. A thousand may fall at my side, and ten thousand at my right hand; but it shall not approach me. I will only look on with my eyes, and see the recompense of the wicked. For I *have made the Lord, my refuge, even the Most High, my dwelling place. No evil will befall me, nor will any plaque come near my tent. For He will give His angels charge concerning me, to guard me in all my ways. They will bear me up in their hands, least I strike my foot against a stone. I will tread upon the lion and cobra, the young lion and the serpent I will trample down. Because I have loved Him, therefore He will deliver me; He will set me securely on high, because I have known His name. I will call upon Him, and He will answer me; He will be with me in trouble; He will rescue me, and honor me. With a long life He will satisfy me, and let me behold His salvation.'* (Psalm 91 with slight modification to make it as a prayer, or read it as is from your Bible).

- **The Lord's Prayer:**

"Our Father who art in heaven, hallowed be Thy name. Thy kingdom come. Thy will be done, on earth as it is in heaven. Give us this day our daily bread. And forgive us our debts as we forgive our debtors. And do not lead us into temptation, but deliver us from evil. For Thine is the kingdom, and power, and the glory, forever. Amen." (Matthew 6:9-13)

- *Revival prayer:*

'Our Heavenly Father, in the name of Your Son, Jesus Christ, hear this prayer of our petition before Your face. We repent for the sins of people in our (town, city, county, or state) and ask for Your mercy, forgiveness and salvation because of Your name and Your glory. We are aware that the people have sinned against You and Your laws and Your commandments. We repent for all the sins which have been committed by (town, city, county, or state): fornication, adultery, homosexuality, all sorts of sexual abominations, pornography, divorces, all kind of human trafficking and abuse, extortions, murders, abortions, hatred, jealousies, envy, covetousness, love of money, revelry, contentions, drunkenness, smoking, drug use, idolatry,

uncleanness, lewdness, sorcery, outbursts of wrath, evil speech, and all kind of abomination and unrighteousness in Your sight.

Also, we repent for the sins of our church, for we have sinned, and have committed iniquity, and have done wickedly, and have rebelled by departing from Your precepts and from Your judgements, from Your Word and from Your commandments. We have forgotten to be your bondservants and went after our own follies and each our own ways. We repent for allowing in our midst all sorts of sexual immorality, divorces, partiality, hypocrisy, all sort of uncleanness, extortions, murders, abortions, hatred, jealousies, envy, covetousness, revelry, contentions, drunkenness, smoking, outbursts of wrath, gossip and evil speech. We repent for our spiritual laziness for forgetting to be the salt and the light of the world, and for using other sources for studying Your Word and putting aside our true source of the truth – Your Holy Bible. We repent for allowing false doctrines to enter in our midst. We repent for rejecting the Holy Spirit and doing everything on our own. We repent that on our post many souls are slipping away into hell while we are busy following and proving our agendas. We repent for not fasting and praying for the lost.

We thank You for Your Son's blood and His redeeming sacrifice. We thank You for by Your mercy we haven't been destroyed yet. We thank You for Your Holy Word and the work of the Holy Spirit. We thank You for the physical blessings You have been pouring out on our country. We thank you for Your providence with food, clean water, clothing, shelter, and peace. We give thanks for all men and rulers of (town, city, county, or state), bless them and help them to seek You and pass moral laws, so that we may lead a quiet and peaceable life in all godliness and reverence. Lord of the harvest, please send out laborers into Your harvest and in our churches, schools, higher education institutions, nursing homes, hospitals, and our homes, for this is good and acceptable in the sight of God our Savior, for You desire all men to be saved and to come to knowledge of the truth. For Christ Jesus is the only one God and one Mediator between God and men, who gave Himself a ransom for all.

We realize, that we are weak but You are strong, we are fallen and without You we can do nothing. We humbly ask You to hear our prayer and supplication and answer us because of Your Son's sacrifice and Your mercy. Please, forgive us and pour out Your Spirit and move Your way amongst us for salvation of many. Give us unity, strength to persevere, faith, and ability and willingness to serve You with no compromises, prayer and fasting. Amen.'

- **Psalm 23:1-4** (Good during the time of hardship)

"The Lord is my shepherd, I shall not want. He makes me lie down in green pastures; He leads me beside quiet waters. He restores my soul; He guides me in the paths of righteousness for His name's sake. Even though I walk through the valley of shadow of death, I fear no evil; for Thou art with me; Thy rod and Thy staff, they comfort me."

- **Psalm 25:4-7, 16-22** (Good during the time of hardship)

"Make me know Thy ways, O Lord; teach me Thy paths. Lead me in Thy truth and teach me, for Thou art the God of my salvation; for Thee I wait all the day. Remember, O Lord, Thy compassion and Thy loving kindnesses, for they have been from of old. Do not remember the sins of my youth or my transgressions; according to Thy loving kindness remember Thou me, for Thy goodness' sake, O Lord. Turn to me and be gracious to me, for I am lonely and afflicted. The troubles of my heart are enlarged; bring me out of my distresses. Look upon my affliction and my trouble, and forgive all my sins. Look upon my enemies, for they are many; and they hate me with violent hatred. Guard my soul and deliver me; do not let me be ashamed, for I take refuge in Thee. Let integrity and uprightness preserve me, for I wait for Thee. Redeem Israel, O God, out of all his trouble."

About the Author

Natalya Vazemiller is personally involved in daily intercessory prayer and Bible study. She wrote her book to share her experience and knowledge of warfare for all women. Natalya is a wife and mother of two homeschooled boys and lives in South Carolina. At the time of writing the book, Natalya was residing in Wisconsin.

Useful Resources

I find these resources useful, but may not agree with everything the authors teach and stand by. Also, by listing them, I do not suggest that I agree or know their theological standing. I found these resources useful enough to list them here for your use. As always, use what works and is agreeable and disregard the rest.

- *"Needless Casualties of War" by John Paul Jackson*
  If one wishes to be binding and commanding the spiritual dark forces, one must read this book. It is easier to get hurt than be useful when one prays in the wrong way.

- *"The Kneeling Christian" by An Unknown Christian*
  This is a great book on prayer.

- *"Guardians of the Great Commission" (the story of women in modern missions) by Ruth A. Tucker*
  This is a great historical account of the women, who have proclaimed the Good News. Read it and get inspired. I hope, God will raise many more great women missionaries for His kingdom advancement.

- *"Tortured for Christ" by Rev. Richard Wurmbrand*
  The Christian classics written by the founder of The Voice of the Martyrs. Reading this book is going to change your service to the Lord and you will pray for the persecuted church in earnest.

- www.nogreaterjoy.org

This website has many resources and tips for your marriage and child raising. It has been very useful in my child raising. They have bimonthly newsletters or magazines full of great support in family affairs and always up to date to the demands of today's day. Books to consider by the organization:

- *"Created to Be His Help Meet"* (Discover how God can make your marriage glorious) by Debi Pearl
- *"Sara Sue Really Learns to Yell & Tell"* & *"Samuel Learns to Yell & Tell"* (A warning for children against sexual predators) both by Debi Pearl
- *"Training Children to Be Strong in Spirit"* by Michael Pearl
- *"To Train Up a Child"* by Michael & Debi Pearl
- *"Jumping Ship"* (What to do so your children don't jump ship to the world when they get older) by Michael & Debi Pearl

- Books for older boys reading by Bob Schultz:
  - "Boyhood and Beyond" (Practical Wisdom for Becoming a Man)
  - "Practical Happiness" (A Young Man's Guide to a Contented Life)
  - "Everyday Battles" (Knowing God Through Our Daily Conflicts)
  - "Created for Work" (Practical Insights for Young Men)